D0366172

MAKE THINGS BETTER

The Path to Success in Business

John Keyser

Copyright © 2020 by John P. Keyser

All rights reserved. No part of this publication may be reproduced, distributed, or transmitted in any form or by any means, including photocopying, recording, or other electronic or mechanical methods, without the prior written permission of the publisher, except in the case of brief quotations embodied in critical reviews and certain other non-commercial uses permitted by copyright law. For permission requests, write to the author, addressed "Attention: Permissions" at johnpkeyser@gmail.com.

John P. Keyser

Glen Ellyn, IL, USA

www.commonsenseleadership.com

Ordering Information:

For details, contact johnpkeyser@gmail.com.

Print ISBN: 978-1-09832-312-7

eBook ISBN: 978-1-09832-313-4

Printed in the United States of America on SFI Certified paper.

First Edition

PREVIOUS BOOKS BY JOHN KEYSER

Make Way For Women: Men and Women Leading Together
Improve Culture and Profits

Published 2015
Written With Adrienne Hand

When Leadership Improves, Everyone Wins:
A Discussion of the Principles of Highly Effective Leadership

Published 2018

ENDORSEMENTS

Drawing on his extensive experience in business, John Keyser offers a practical and hope-filled guide to successful leadership. Keyser's vision is balanced, placing family before work, while acknowledging work's demands, and emphasizing other values such as humility and self-effacing community spirit. Keyser's advice will bear rich fruit in any walk of life.

> – Sister Mary Samuel Handwerker, O.P., Co-Foundress of Dominican Sisters of Mary Mother of the Eucharist, Ann Arbor

This book is not only an excellent guide for a successful business career, but also for a successful life, including family and personal relationships. It aligns beautifully with my own Christian values and is a playbook for creating a better world, particularly in these uncertain times.

> – Jerry Paga, CPA and Retired Chief Financial Officer

This book is timely. A common sense guide on how to be an effective leader through constant communication and open dialogue. The principles John enumerates throughout really resonate and take hold. Thank you, John!

> – Susan Mahanor, Everest Insurance

John and I worked together for 20 years at Johnson & Higgins. Part of that time he was my boss, later we were Partners. Before John brought me into J & H, he was my broker, servicing the risk management objectives at my previous company. In all instances, his leadership and business acumen followed the path he has outlined in this, his most recent book. These methods for building relationships with our people and our clients that worked so successfully for us then are still relevant in today's changing business climate and are a roadmap for success. Leadership, humility, empathy, teamwork, collaboration, listening, and communicating are critical skills in business, which this book validates.

– Norman Barham, Former President, Johnson & Higgins

In this helpful guide Keyser offers great practical advice for the person seeking to lead. Focusing on relationship, humility, and self-sacrifice, Keyser lays out a straightforward framework that would apply to leadership both secular and spiritual. As he notes, leadership is not the same as being talented, but involves cultivating relationships to motivate and activate the talents of those around you. His approach is holistic and exudes a strong spirituality that would not be overly burdensome to the secular reader.

– Fr. Matt Litak, MDiv, STB, Archdiocese of Chicago

John Keyser's third book builds on the tenets of his earlier important work. What strikes me is how simple John makes this for those at any stage of their career—these classic, repeatable principles lay the foundation for success in business and in life. Just imagine what we could accomplish if we asked ourselves at day's end if we made just one thing *better*?!

– Matt Wey, Managing Director, Marsh & McLennan

John Keyser's new book, *Make Things Better: The Path to Success in Business*, offers essential and practical advice for executives, managers and team members. Its first three words should become the goal of every workplace interaction—make things better. John's book offers the hands-on guidance of a successful business executive—one who knows how to lead and develop people. The book's power is in the clarity, simplicity and relevance of its advice—try always to be early, questions are our best friends, strive for improvement. Every reader will come away saying—"I can try that, I can do that."

> – Christine LaSala, Chair, Willis Towers Watson North America (Retired)

The title of this book is a common sense ethical imperative to do good work, take initiative, and give priority to relationships in the process of becoming a great manager and leader! The author's experience and wisdom is communicated concisely in stories, examples and lessons for the post pandemic and highly technology world.

> – John Fontana, Co-Director, Ignatian Fellows Program, Loyola University of Chicago, and Fontana Leadership Development

REGARDLESS OUR POSITION, WE CAN ALL BE LEADERS BY CONTRIBUTING IDEAS AND HELPING MAKE THINGS BETTER

TABLE OF CONTENTS

WITH GREAT APPRECIATION

I am very fortunate, as I grew up with a loving and fun family and now continue to be blessed with loving family and friends, some new, and many who are long time and even go back to our school days. Some I mention have helped with this book; others are friends who have helped form me with their friendship and in many instances are role models for me.

This book has been written at our dining room table in beautiful Charlevoix, Michigan and in Glen Ellyn, Illinois, and in the library of both towns; well, also in a few coffee shops.

My wife, Kerry, is a source of ideas, edits, and inspiration. No way could I have completed this book without her love and support. I am blessed indeed. Kerry's background is clinical psychology and she is a spiritual director in the church. She understands people and their feelings and is a continued source of motivation to me in our everyday lives, and certainly with my thinking and writing. Every business and every academic and religious organization we work with are "people businesses," and every people business is about relationships.

My mom and dad and sister, Carol, are no longer with us, yet they are firmly in my heart and mind, as are my sisters, Noel and Kelly. Actually, Kelly is my sister-in-law, though we believe we are sister and brother.

I have a special place in my heart for my children, Kevin and Leigh, and their mother, Liz. They are exceptional and I thank God for them, and for my three grandsons, Carter, Mason, and Nevin, to whom I am "Grandpops." I have great appreciation for my daughter-in-law, Jovana, and Ziv Lalich, my son-in-law. They are upstanding, loving, and highly accomplished. I also have enormous fondness for my nephews, Will and Graham Arensen.

Marisa Peacock, an internet-marketing specialist extraordinaire, has been an enormous help to me with this book, and I am very appreciative. Without Marisa, no book. She is competent, talented, and helpful.

I am grateful for the Georgetown University Institute for Transformational Leadership from which I gained a wealth of knowledge and ideas in studying leadership, as well as from my colleagues who also are graduates of the program. We are a generous and sharing community.

I consider my fellow leadership coaches, Carylynn Larson, Sally Seppanen, Lulu Gonella, Clay Parcells, Cari Sisserson, Melissa Fennell Kessler, and Phil Holberton as colleagues as we are quick to share ideas, feedback, and helpful information.

I have gained great insight from working with clients, including Peter Hill, Alex Elmore, and many others at Billy Casper Golf, the leader in the golf course management field, and a close-knit, caring, and exceptional group of professionals. My work with Albertus Magnus College in New Haven has been thrilling, as Marc Camille, Andrea Kovacs, and Sean O'Connell exemplify humility and dedication in serving their team members and other colleagues to the very best of their abilities and they continue to grow in their leadership, which is already highly effective.

We are privileged to support a number of dioceses and churches, their priests and staffs, in helping them strive for continuous improvement of leadership, their own and their team's. It is especially rewarding to be in conversation with a number of priests who are exceptional, care deeply about being in service to others, and are open and dedicated to continuing to learn and grow to be the best version of themselves as priests and leaders.

At the risk of unintentionally omitting someone(s), I do wish to identify people who have had a favorable impact on me going way back and right up to currently. As friends, each means a lot. They are special and I look upon them and their character with huge admiration. Some have passed, yet are still very much in my mind and heart.

I grew up in Westhampton Beach on Long Island with the McCafferys, McBrides, McCarthys, Morgans, Kennys, Owens, Dwyers, and Auers, all upstanding and caring families, and Lou Clarke, Connie Walsh, Gerry Seitz, and others.

Great friends from the Bronxville, N.Y. area include the McNally, Mullen, Ward, Rizzo, DiMenna, Warble, Reilly, and Hoyt families; and from Winnetka, Illinois Pat and Mardi Hackett, Gerry and Kathy Egan, and the Hickey family.

I had the good fortunate to be educated and formed by the Jesuits at Georgetown University, and I especially mention Fr. Bob Lawton, S.J. and Fr. Leo O'Donovan, S.J., two outstanding priests and leaders.

Fellow Georgetown graduates and their spouses I greatly admire include Michael and Maureen Gibbons, Rob and Mimi Cullen, Jack and Jackie Mariano, Charlie and Colette Russell and family, Mark Williams and family, Jim and Diane Duffy and family, Tom Begley, Mike Sheehan, Neil Hartigan, Pete Kelly, Tom Kramer, Art and Joan Connolly, Peter Somma, Strat and Kathy Wallace, Ed Baran, Larry McGivney, Irene and Ed Shaw, Ray Drymalski, John Walker, Jake Styacich, Murphy and Meagan Gallagher, Chris Golski, Christy Larrimore, Connie Isler, Taylor Price, George Wetzel, Bruce Keller, Jeff Chapski, Ed Machir, Christine Brown-Quinn, Ted Laborde, Paul Reardon, Eric Sullivan, Roger O'Neal, Joe Tuthill, Rick DeBobes, Don Hudenburg, JohnMolloy, Wally Maher, Dick Milone, Pat O'Donnell, Mike O'Connor, Lou Kiefer, Walter Hickey, Bill McBride, Bob Adelberg, Vince Manahan, Paul Fitzgerald, Skip Lennon, Dick Barry, Jack McGarty—and I could continue literally for pages.

Outstanding role models from Georgetown University itself include Rob Sgarlata, Brian Weise, outstanding football and men's soccer coaches, respectfully; Sarah Rawls Thompson and Emily White Hull, when they were with the alumni association; Patrick Kilcarr, who has been a treasure for the university and it's students for years; Bob Bies, an exceptional professor of management and leadership; and Fr. Mark Bosco, S.J., who is responsible for Georgetown's very special Campus Ministry programs.

Lew Perry was my very favorite teacher from high school, the epitome of a gentleman, whom I stayed in touch with until he was in his 90s.

Special friends from Charlevoix, Michigan are Mary Plude, Kathleen Dvorcek, Kendall Hayes, Fr. Peter Wigton, Leilani Durbin, Amber Parsons Munday, Gretchen Bartelli, Laura Kelly, the Golski family, the Mannions, MacCarthys, Larimores, Buntins, Paynes, Dan Hales, Bob Klein, Jerry Paga, and the Cook and Romeyn families.

Other friends and role models are John and Becky Halleron, Adrienne Hand (who got me started writing, while my English professors probably rolled over in their graves), John Fontana, Bill Curtis and Sue Mahanor, Rebecca Johnson, Amanda and Matt Doyle, Sarah and Andy Funt, Fr Tim Daniel, Sr Mary Samuel Handwerker, Pam Evanson, Bert and Sandi Getz, Colette Kleitz, Dave Edmonds, Brian Gray, Eduardo Gerlein, Meaghan Canton Feder, Al Ritter, Afy Shahidi, Bud and Mary Jane O'Connor, Angela Zeng, Ken Tyrrell, Steve Ingham, Garrett Hughes, Mary Mavis (who was my coach, and a great one, when I was with Johnson & Higgins), Dr. Perry Cammisa and Dr. Natalia Ivanchenko, who take good care of us, and our neighbors the Lysaghts, Youmans, and Hodgsons.

Much of my career was with Johnson & Higgins, which after 154 years became part of Marsh & McLennan, sadly for many. Again, I could write a book about the ladies and gentlemen—team players—who I worked with at J&H. People whose influence I continue to especially value are

Dick Purnell, Bill Dunn, Dick Meyer, Massie Valentine, Norm Barham, Christine LaSala, Betsy Balderston, Gardner Mundy, Dan Knise, Mike Crowley, Matt Wey, John Gussenhoven, Paul Charlesworth, Mike Epstein, Don Price, Kathy Wernet, Kim Johnson, Larry Lund, Sharon Alexander, Jim Appleton, Jim Wylie, Ferd Baruch, Larry Geneen, Mike Turpin, and I have to mention Cathy Becker, an exceptional HR specialist, and someone who definitely understands what good leadership looks like, and who exemplifies strong character values.

I thank God for the blessing of having these people and others in my life. They mean the world to me

NOTE TO MY READERS

The chapters in this book are reminders of leadership principles. They are not in order of importance, as I believe all have significant value and will help with our success as a teammate and leader.

I repeat many of the ideas and principles throughout the chapters, including these:

- Whatever our field, we are in a people business.
- Striving for improvement is the path to success.
- Managers focus on numbers; leaders focus first on people.
- Conversations are the work of a leader.
- A problem discussed is a problem half-solved.
- The best ideas are bottom up ideas; we want ideas to flow up.
- We can all learn from one another.
- Happy employees do better work.
- A short conversation is better than no conversation.
- Ask what success looks like for each project or assignment.

More and more people are working remotely, which only makes the emphasis of this book about the vital importance of relationships all the more challenging. Yet our success depends on our relationships, and we each have to commit to doing the best we can to stay in touch, letting our colleagues (including our manager, peers, direct reports, and other colleagues) know of our genuine care for them, and we cannot do this simply through email. We all receive so many emails, some of us in the hundreds each day. Thus, it is important that we pick up the phone and/or send a hand-written note—and a short conversation or brief note is better than no conversation or note. A text can be helpful, unless they become too plentiful. Right now, I feel they can be effective, even just "I am thinking about you. How are you?"

If we and/or our team members are remote, let's be sure to stay connected, maybe with FaceTime or Zoom conversations. Also, if we are remote, think about how often we should visit our home office and whom we should visit with. I worked with one person who was in sales, and was good at it, but was not appropriately connected with his team members. He tended to give orders. People did not have much respect for him or a desire to work with him. And he viewed a quarterly visit to his home office as a burden. In my opinion, if he wants to be successful, he should look to visit with his team members and the home office more often, not less, which is where he is right now. He is keeping his job for now because of his sales record, but I expect advancement is not in the cards for him, and sales tends to be a younger person's job versus someone in his 50s or 60s. I feel he is being short-sighted.

For those who are spiritual, I offer that you need not hide this. Spirituality can bring us together, bring us closer. This is not promoting our religion. Religions at times can keep us divided, while not so with spirituality.

All of us have times, often frequently, when we are weighed down heavily in our hearts, whether from stress, an overbearing issue in our work, a challenging or depressing relationship, or an illness, our own or that of a family member or friend. We can offer to pray for our colleague, or even offer to pray *with* our colleague. I have seen how moved and appreciative someone is when another has softly prayed with them for their intention.

While business is not for the faint of heart, with some sacrifice at times, I believe we can succeed, love our work, have a balanced life style, and have a satisfying career if we follow the principles and practices offered in this book.

1

INTRODUCTION

WHY I AM WRITING THIS BOOK

This book is written for everyone in business, people of all levels within their company, including those in small businesses, with the hope that this may encourage people to step up, contribute their ideas, and help make good things happen within their company; it could be said to go beyond simply their job description.

Simply doing our job very well may not lead to the success we are capable of.

There are a great many good people who may be hesitant to step out of their comfort zone, perhaps they may not have a high level of inner confidence. However, that does not mean that they have any less potential than those who are confident. Not at all.

I think of people I know who are highly intelligent, dedicated, conscientious, and selfless. They are great team members, and they could contribute even more in their work and as leaders.

I believe the principles offered in this book will also be helpful to those in small businesses. Many people in small businesses do not have the benefit of training programs, or having the advantage of helpful mentors to share wisdom and experience.

So, here's my third book, written solely to share ideas which I hope and pray will help talented, dedicated, good people reach the potential they desire in business and as leaders.

Everyone can be a leader, and I encourage us all to positively influence our colleagues and companies to do outstanding work, to collaborate, have enjoyable work environments, and be successful.

What I propose in this book is simple, and simple is good. It's common sense. Hopefully, as you read through the chapters you will nod in agreement, and maybe highlight ideas that speak to you, that you feel make sense. They may simply be reminders, yet they are needed reminders.

Many of the people I feel could be further along in their companies and their careers will benefit from these ideas.

I do not think advancing is playing "company politics" or that promoting one's accomplishments are paths to advancement. Rather, success comes from doing excellent work, being a great teammate, contributing ideas for improvement, helping make good things happen (e.g., saving time and expenses), and helping one's company grow.

I will discuss in a later chapter that anyone in any position can help their company. An administrative assistant, an intern, or a receptionist can meet someone at a church function, a party, or any gathering and be alert to how their company might serve this person's business and simply ask if they could arrange for an executive or someone appropriate to have a conversation with them or someone they designate.

A person who initiates a growth opportunity, a savings, or an idea that benefits their company, will turn the heads of the senior executives. I know firsthand. When I was a very junior employee of a large company in New York City, I went to a luncheon and happened to sit next to someone from a Fortune 100 company. We had a good conversation, and got together again a few weeks later. When we did, I asked if we could have a meeting at which I could bring several selected people from my company who could help explore their needs and whether or not we might be helpful and assist them. Praise God, it all worked out and we had a new client, and people appreciated my initiating the opportunity.

Not to say that bringing in a new client(s) is the answer to being promoted. Not at all. There are many fundamentals we must do and do well. Many of these are discussed in the various chapters. And, as stated above, they really are fundamental. They include:

- Doing excellent work
- Clarifying what success looks like for each project or assignment
- Being a great teammate
- Having a positive attitude
- Maintaining a wholesome working relationship with one's boss, teammates, direct reports, and other colleagues
- Being encouraging and positive
- Asking how we can help

If we want to be a leader and succeed, we likely can. We must have the right attitude. Attitude is everything. And we must be humble and selfless, wanting our company to be a great place to work and wanting our team members and other colleagues to do great work and succeed.

We want to be appreciated by our teammates for our help and contributions, and for our being a source of positive energy—for the difference we make.

The saying, "find something you love to do and you never have to work a day in your life," is generally true. I was fortunate. For much of my working career, I was with great people and we worked hard, were unselfish, were all about the team, and we had a blast. We all had unique strengths, we worked well together, and treated one another with respect and a genuine fondness.

We were a bunch of people who made things happen. We didn't seek credit or the spotlight; we simply did what was needed to assure happy clients… and happy teammates.

I hope this book is widely read so that deserving people advance as leaders and enjoy their work and being part of their company.

We need more capable leaders in our businesses. Morale is generally not good in many—maybe most—companies across the country. Let's do our very best to change that.

2

EVERYONE CAN BE A LEADER

Leadership does not come from our title or our corner office, it comes from our influence. We all, no matter our position or experience, have the ability to influence. We can encourage, teach, and coach a teammate, and this is leadership. We can appropriately offer feedback, be it positive or constructive and helpful, and this is leadership.

Keys to having the influence to support others is having a genuine interest in helping them, being selfless, and having a real desire to see others be successful.

It must be done quietly, without seeking credit. We do not seek personal credit. We share credit.

We, of course, want to do excellent work ourselves, and we want to embody an attitude of being all about the team. We want our success to come from the combined success of the team, a team that collaborates and enthusiastically shares information and helps one another – a team that is inclusive – and everyone contributes, without fear of being put down – everyone is sharing ideas for improvement, wanting to help make things better.

As a leader, we embrace a positive, optimistic, enthusiastic attitude. We never talk about someone behind her back. We avoid office politics and internal competition.

Looking to be a good influence on everyone in our company is of paramount importance, and it must be everyone, of all levels. Everyone is important and everyone's work is important. Try to have conversations and good relationships with people throughout our company, those above us and those below us.

Help people feel appreciated and valued and that their work matters, as do their ideas.

Leadership is how we help people feel about themselves, which I mention throughout this book. I also often mention that managers focus on numbers, while leaders focus first on people.

No matter our position, we can do excellent work ourselves and also help our team members and other colleagues do excellent work themselves.

Often in these chapters, we discuss the great value of feedback, and that there is an art to offering timely and honest feedback to help another develop. There also is an art to receiving feedback appreciatively, realizing that every one of us have areas of potential improvement.

There is also feedforward, which is offering suggestions to change the future for the better, and can be conversations with someone to help her success going forward. At times, feedforward can be easier to offer than feedback, as there is less tendency for a person to be defensive and rationalize. That said, please do not avoid offering feedback, as it can be helpful. Both feedback and feedforward can offer significant value.

We each can make a positive difference in our company, to make things better, and help people be their very best.

3

LEADERS MAKE THINGS BETTER

Leaders make things better, and so do great team members.

- When we see a problem, we don't ignore it or complain; we try to fix it.

- We ask our manager how we may help her.

- And the same is true with our team members, we ask how we may help.

- As we are seeking to offer ideas that may improve our work and our company, we encourage our teammates to offer their ideas as well. The quantity of ideas is important, just as is the quality of ideas. The more ideas, the more likely is improvement

- We offer timely and honest feedback to our manager, teammates, and other colleagues:

  - Feedback that is positive, such as: "You did a great job at the meeting this morning when you asked everyone for their ideas and for us to please be honest."

  - Feedback that is constructive, such as "May I share feedback which I hope will be helpful? At this morning's meeting, I felt we would have been appreciative if you asked each of us how we felt about the ideas you put forth."

There is an art to offering feedback. This is an art worth learning, and when we do, we will have the confidence to do it well. Just stating our positive intent upfront goes a long way. And there is an art to accepting feedback with appreciation and a desire to learn, recognizing there likely is truth in the feedback.

We are all well-advised to learn the art of effective feedback, both offering and receiving.

Leaders understand that their success comes from the success of their people. If we, as a team member, embody that same attitude, then we succeed as a team, and a "one for all and all for one" attitude will have a very positive effect on the spirit and culture of our company. Very likely, our unselfish, positive attitude will be noticed and appreciated.

Do we want to be a leader, who is someone that helps others do well and succeed? It requires time, effort, and sacrifice. We cannot be watching the clock and counting hours. If we view our job as 9 to 5, it is not likely we'll advance to higher levels.

In facilitating a 360 Leadership Assessment for a regional manager, his boss disappointingly told me that the person had never come to him and asked, "What more can I do to help you?" Not once. The boss concludes, "He will only do what he feels he has to do, and does not reach out to help others." He does not want to volunteer to take on more work, nor does he seem to want to help his manager. That is his choice, and it will certainly limit his opportunity to move ahead.

Please do not get me wrong. I promote a balanced lifestyle, and that our faith, our family, our health, and our friends are more important than our work. We need quality time outside of our work. We need time with our spouse or significant other, our children, our aging parents. It's not to work until all hours.   But we must appreciate that our work and career are important as well, and business requires hard work and, at times, sacrifice. This comes with the territory.

We can work hard, make the sacrifices, and still make most of our children's ball games, plays, concerts, and teacher meetings. It is actually a little easier today than it was in the past, thanks to technology. We can stay connected now, and a great many companies are flexible to help people with their family and other personal needs.

Generally, it is those who do excellent work, help others do excellent work, and help their company succeed who advance. Of course, character values matter. Being selfless and caring about others—our colleagues, clients, and those in our communities—models good character values.

There are exceptions, when people are promoted by someone who does not *understand that leadership is absolutely about helping the team succeed.* This must be made clear. As a leader, our success comes from the success of our team members. People who do not understand and embody this are not likely to continue to rise within their company.

When I was with Johnson & Higgins, our Chairman and CEO, Dick Purnell, who was one of the most honorable people I have ever known, had a plaque prominently on the wall of his office: "There is no limit to how far someone can go if she does not seek personal credit." This was contagious, and purveyed our organizational culture. We were collaborative and rooted for one another. We exemplified the power of a true team.

If we do excellent work, help others do the same, help make our team's and company's culture positive, enthusiastic and collaborative, we will very likely advance. Our leadership will be needed for the difference we make.

Be a team player by helping others do excellent work and achieve success. We will be admired and appreciated, including by those above us, for sharing our gift of leadership. Leadership is, indeed, a gift we can all enjoy.

We want to offer our help as we can, and if we are more experienced and/ or knowledgeable than others, we could offer to mentor or coach them.

Successful business executives share about the great benefit they received earlier in their careers from a more senior leader in their company who took the time to mentor them.

In my former company, I can think of any number of great people who had the benefit of the interest and attention given to them by our department managers, office managers, regional managers, and executive committee members, who were virtually all servant leaders and role models. People were succeeding in good part thanks to this mentoring. It was fun to be a part of such a culture.

Those who are ambitious and eager to advance and be successful within our company or field would be well-advised to realize the importance of taking control of their career. We cannot wait to be chosen. We well might not be. Rather, we could seek out a mentor ourselves, someone we respect for their knowledge, experience, judgment, and accomplishments. If the situation is right, they could well be honored to be asked, and ultimately if they are impressed with our commitment, they could choose to be an advocate/sponsor for us when opportunities become available.

Should a woman seek a woman to be her mentor, and a man another man, or someone of the same race? No, that should not be an issue. Seek to choose the person we feel will be best to guide us.

Also, realize that the best mentor may not be within our company. Rather, that person could be within our industry, or could even be someone we admire for their character and judgment. That can work as well.

What could mentoring look like? Mentoring is a genuine commitment to helping the development of perhaps a less knowledgeable and less experienced colleague. At its best, mentoring is a collaboration that is truly shared, enriching the lives of both. Done well by both the mentor and mentee, the relationship will have an important impact and result in significantly enhancing the mentee's effectiveness.

There is no one set approach to mentoring. It works best when mentors feel a strong sense of responsibility and have an attitude of truly wanting to help with another's success. Mentoring works especially well when the relationship is "organic," that is, when two people naturally form an informal but intentional relationship. Both parties have an obligation and need to speak up promptly if this is not working as one of them would like.

The tone of the relationship is important. The capacity of the mentor to influence rests heavily on her ability to relate in a non-authoritative way, while guiding the mentee's learning and growth.

It is helpful to begin with an assessment of the mentee's competencies and areas of potential growth, for example:

- Readiness to be mentored?
- Receptivity to us as a mentor?
- Does she have self-awareness and relationship management intelligence?
- Can she articulate her strengths and her vulnerabilities?
- Is she receptive to hearing about potential blind spots and biases?

Ideally, we and the person we will mentor both have the humility to be vulnerable and will honestly share thoughts about potential areas of growth.

Mentoring works best when the person is ready, accepts that seeking to become better is a strength—a great strength—and certainly not a weakness, and has the motivation and drive to work toward specific goals.

If this works as intended—and it certainly can if we commit to it and follow through—there should be personal satisfaction and fulfillment for us, as mentor, and as well for the mentee. By helping bring out the best in a person, she will have a greater ability to be a leader, a great teammate, and to have a positive effect on organizational culture and our company's success.

Additional guidelines for mentoring:

- Set expectations and goals together.
- Be open and honest with each other about progress, and how the relationship is working.
- Recognize that there must be compatibility, respect, trust, and available time.
- Trust can be enhanced if both we and our mentee are comfortable allowing ourselves to be vulnerable with one another.
- As a mentor, recognize the need to be both encouraging and challenging.

It is certainly true that everyone is already busy. Taking on a mentoring relationship is an added and important responsibility. Yet even a small-time commitment can reap huge rewards. We will discover a deep sense of satisfaction, and we will likely further enhance our own feedback and relationships skills, and continue our own learning and growth. We can all learn from one another—an important principle of a healthy organizational culture.

Being a mentor does not come with recognition. Definitely not. There should be none. We do it selflessly, as we want to be helpful, to share our gifts and insight with another(s). Yet, done well, it brings us self-satisfaction.

Is there a person or people who we see in our company, at our church, at places we volunteer, and/or in our community, who we respect and feel has the potential to be a leader? Could we be the leader who could help unlock that potential?

Leaders raise up other leaders.

4

HUMILITY IS THE FOUNDATION OF GROWTH

The first test of a truly great person is his humility.

– John Ruskin

When we admit our own imperfections, we make ourselves more approachable. Our humility invites real conversations with others, regardless of their title or position. It enables us to see the value of seeking ideas and to be appreciative, receptive, and open-minded.

Humility leads to gratitude, and it cultivates respect. This sets the tone for great teamwork and a winning organizational culture, as humility drives out the isolating tendencies of pride, cultivates unity, and brings out the power of a team. This is what we want to strive for.

When I was fortunate to be in leadership roles myself, and now as I support and help leaders, I continually see that the companies with healthy organizational cultures are ones built not with superstars but rather with people who do good work, are humble, have solid character values, and are great teammates. Their humility is attractive and enables strong relationships internally and externally with clients.

If we are good, we don't have to tell anyone we are. We will be admired for our modesty and our integrity. People will gravitate towards us and there will be a natural ease of respectful conversations.

When we are humble, we see our need for growth. We are able to improve our leadership abilities when we:

- Realize that asking for help is a sign of strength.
- Help others learn, grow, and succeed.
- Are comfortable sharing credit for success, and shine the spotlight on others.
- Accept responsibility when things do not go well

By asking for help and feedback, we demonstrate an inner confidence that is appealing to others. Expressing what we are working on in our own development and how we are hoping to improve inspires others to do the same.

When we invite others to improve alongside us, we set in motion a powerful culture change. We open up thinking and invite everyone to learn from one another as we build trust and foster unity among team members. We become patient with the development needs of others and are able to help turn seemingly "failed" situations into opportunities for growth and insight.

When there is humility among team members, we see people seeking the good in one another and the team, and healthy, respectful, honest, and growth-producing communication that honors the contributions of everyone.

Simply put, humility is the foundation for personal, team, and corporate growth.

I listened to a presentation about humility by Kris Vallotton of Bethel Church in California. He offered these as just some of the inherent practices of people who are humble:

- They rejoice in the success of others.
- No job or work is beneath them.
- They seek advice from others.
- They are teachable, are life-long learners.
- Life to them is about how they help others succeed.
- They are comfortable in their own skin, with who they are.
- They are thankful.

Regardless of our position, let us "lead with humility." That would be a good mantra for us all.

The true test of our humility is manifested in our relationships with others.

PRINCIPLES THAT SERVE US WELL AND LEAD TO SUCCESS

- We can all be leaders.

- Leadership comes from our ability to influence another(s), not from our title.

- Leadership is not about our being great; it is about our helping others be great.

- Conversations are the work of a leader, and a short conversation is better than no conversation.

5

OUR RELATIONSHIPS IMPACT OUR EFFECTIVENESS

Leaders understand the ultimate power of relationships.

– Tom Peters

Early in my career in New York City, I attended a Dale Carnegie training program and found it very helpful. The two fellows who taught our program were amazing. I was totally taken by their quiet confidence, poise, and ability to communicate and tell stories.

Here I am, many years later, and an advocate for reading leadership books like Carnegie's enduring classic, *How to Win Friends and Influence People*, which was written in 1936 and is more relevant today than it was 80-plus years ago.

I encourage executives and up-and-comers to read one leadership book a month for inspiration and ideas. The good news today is that these books tend to be easy reads, maybe 150 to 200 pages, and they often use stories to validate their messages. I always get at least a few ideas and a whole lot of inspiration to eagerly share with those with whom I work.

Like most of us, I love the theory that simple is sensible. That's exactly what *How to Win Friends and Influence People* is, the basics of leadership, and it makes so much sense. In fact, I fervently believe it makes even more sense today than when it was written.

I mention below some of the "golden rules" that are Mr. Carnegie's principles. These were keys to success then, always have been, and just think how vital they are now in our crazy-busy world when so many, unfortunately most, senior managers are nearly consumed with meetings, conference calls, our computers, smart phones, in conversation in the C-suites, and traveling, with many people working remotely, and so much communication is via email.

What would I like to see? I would like our managers regularly having conversations with our external clients, of course, and with our internal clients, the people in our company—all the people, not just with other senior executives.

To be very successful consistently, year after year, leaders must make conversations a daily priority—quality two-way conversations that treat others as teammates and show gratitude and a genuine interest in them.

Think about these golden rules offered by Dale Carnegie. These are just some of his principles in random order, as each is important:

- Don't criticize or complain.
- Give honest, sincere appreciation.
- Be genuinely interested in other people.
- Remember and call people by their name.
- Ask good questions and be an attentive listener.
- Encourage others to share about themselves and their thoughts and feelings.
- Help others feel important, and do it sincerely.
- Show respect for another person's opinions.

- Begin in a friendly way.

- Be encouraging.

- Let others do a great deal of the talking.

- Let people think the ideas are theirs.

- Try to understand what others think and their reasoning.

To me, these are the ABCs of leadership, the fundamentals. If we abide by these rules, with sincerity, because we genuinely care about our colleagues and we are not self-absorbed, those on our teams will be appreciative and be motivated to do their very best work, and going the extra mile when needed.

We must bear in mind the importance of asking open-ended questions, and asking people for their ideas, advice, opinions, input, and feedback. We'll learn a lot and our people will feel grateful.

There is the very effective approach of "leadership by questioning." For example, when someone asks what action we should take, ask that person what she feels are the options and what she recommends, and why. Leadership by questioning helps our people learn and grow. And isn't that our responsibility as a leader, to help others?

The senior leadership team of one company I know has read *How to Win Friends and Influence People* and then had roundtable discussions about the ideas and how to use them to help assure strong relationships.

Yes, leadership can be simple, utilizing the basics of how to treat others and have solid relationships.

Actually, this is why I named our coaching and consulting services company Common Sense Leadership. I credit my coach, Mary Mavis, as she mentioned that my short leadership articles essentially were common sense. That triggered my search to learn if that could be the name of our company, and I was delighted to find it was available.

While business is complicated, and managing our time is challenging, I do believe that leadership is basic—it is common sense: it is following our instincts, doing what is right, making things better, and earning the respect and trust of our people.

Two principles I love are:

- A manager likes to talk; a leader likes to listen.
- A manager thinks first about numbers; while a leader thinks first about people.

I hope these golden rules ring true to you, as they do for me—even more so many years after Carnegie's debut in my life.

Similar to Carnegie's ideas, a priest, leading his people to live virtuous and happy lives, shared this: "The most effective way for us to influence and inspire someone is to develop a relationship with that person and to be a role model, so the person respects our values and our way of being, and wishes to follow our example."

The goal of helping others excel is fundamental to solid, respectful relationships.

Being a role model and leading by example are far more effective than telling someone, "Here's how you should develop effective relationships" or "Here's how you should live."

It can be simple. For example, key principles are:

- Inspire, encourage, teach, mentor, and coach others.

- Know that we have a responsibility to treat others with respect and kindness, and to help them learn, grow, and succeed.

- Give timely and honest feedback—respectful, positive, and also constructive areas of potential improvement. This is what people want.

- Have humility. We are no better and no worse than anyone else.

It's the relationships we develop with our colleagues, and definitely including our manager, that enable us to have a positive influence.

Certainly there is a place for email, to distribute information efficiently. But it is conversations, not emails, that create the path to quality relationships, founded on respect and trust.

Conversations with our colleagues must be a very high priority, definitely including our manager and direct reports, asking purposeful questions and listening to learn and understand.

Just imagine the rich information we'll receive if we regularly ask:

- How could we improve our communication?
- What gets in the way of doing our best work?
- How could I be more helpful to you?
- What do you think should be our priorities going forward?
- What should we be trying to make happen in the next two months?
- What advice do you have for me?

Take notes. It helps us remember and it is a sign of respect. People want to be heard and to feel their ideas matter, and that we care about them and their well-being. So let's make conversations with our colleagues our priority.

Success in business is founded on our relationships.

6

EMOTIONAL INTELLIGENCE IS A KEY INDICATOR OF OUR SUCCESS

Realizing the importance of relationships, we must understand how much our emotional intelligence helps put people at ease, helps us be easy to work with, creates trust, conveys respect, aligns us with others, and furthers a "can-do" attitude.

Note: We refer to emotional intelligence as EQ. In other articles and books, it may be referred to as EI or EQ-i, essentially the same set of skills.

Emotional intelligence is "the single best predictor of performance in the workplace and the strongest driver of leadership and personal excellence," according to Travis Bradberry and Jean Greaves, PhDs, coauthors of *Emotional Intelligence 2.0,* and their extensive research.

Emotional intelligence is that something within us that helps us sense how we feel and enables us to truly connect with others and form strong relationships, founded on admiration, appreciation, and trust. It gives us the desire to be present and listen to someone when they most need it. This has a surprisingly calming effect on both the speaker and the listener.

EQ is that sense of internal balance that enables us to keep our composure, make good decisions, communicate successfully, and continue to work effectively even when under stress.

Four main skill areas of emotional intelligence are:

- Self-awareness—our ability to perceive our emotions and understand our tendencies to act in certain ways in given situations.

- Social awareness—our ability to sense the emotions of other people; in other words, what they are thinking and feeling.

- Self-management—our ability to use awareness of our emotions to stay composed and flexible and to conduct ourselves positively and constructively.

- Relationship management—our ability to use our awareness of our own emotions and those of others to manage interactions successfully.

Some of us are born with a high level of emotional intelligence. Others are not. Many of us are not aware of how our emotions may be adversely affecting our thinking, our actions, and our reactions to others—and in addition, how we are being perceived and received by others.

The good news is that we can learn to increase our emotional intelligence. We can take an online assessment to determine our EQ scores, our levels of emotional intelligence. I highly recommend doing this. If we measure our skill levels, we can work to improve them.

I must mention, however, that the online assessment is self-rated and thus may not be truly accurate. A person I know scored himself extremely high on his EQ and within six months was fired, as he did not have the respect of his team members.

A better way to gain a sense is to humbly ask those who work with us to please offer their honest and thoughtful perceptions and advice and that we will be appreciative.

The most effective approach is a 360 Leadership Assessment, if it is done well. Unfortunately, many are simply an online questionnaire and lack the follow-through coaching necessary to help a person change long-ingrained habits and discuss their blind spots. A good 360 Leadership Assessment can be truly transformative in our growth. It was for me personally.

When we grow in our effective use of our EQ, we increase our ability to develop more solid, trusting relationships. This is so helpful, as success in business and leadership is grounded on our relationships.

Our internal relationships—the ones we have with our manager, direct reports, team members, and other colleagues—can make or break us! They can make or break our team and our company.

With high EQ, we can actively support and help others succeed, which can be contagious throughout our company.

We do this when we can by lifting our heads from our laptops and smart-phones, setting down our files, coming around our desk, and stepping out of our office to have conversations with co-workers. When we reach out to others and humbly and earnestly learn about their challenges and support them, we actually reduce our own stress in addition to theirs.

If we are not working at the same location, we can speak by phone, FaceTime, or Zoom.

EQ is about our effectiveness in working with others. People will want to work with us, to follow us, if we are empathetic, caring, focused on the success and well-being of others, without a personal agenda, and we listen with sincere interest.

The most productive organizational cultures are those with women active in senior leadership. While there are many exceptions, women, in general, have an overall emotional intelligence that is higher than that of men. In fact, women generally score a little higher on self-management, social awareness, and relationship management, while the scores of men and women on self-awareness tend to be about equal.

Women's relationship skills and relationship awareness are assets to building trust and collaboration.

As an example, a female senior executive told me, "I think it is very important to be able to pick up on the motivational and emotional cues of those around me. I work very hard at noticing the moods and needs of my team members to help keep them 'up' and to help them maximize their potential." This is a person who leads with her heart.

Research by TalentSmart, the organization Bradberry and Greaves founded and a recognized leader in the emotional intelligence field, reveals that a great many businesspeople do not feel respected and valued. This has a massive negative effect on organizational cultures.

People should be promoted to senior positions because of how effective they will be as leaders, not because of what they know and how long they have been with us. One may be very good at sales, marketing, finance, or information technology, for example, but effective leadership requires a different set of skills. Does the candidate realize that? Does she want to develop these skills and accept the fact that it will no longer about her own success; it will be now about her team members and the team's success?

EQ is more important to leadership performance than any other skill—a lot more important.

The path to succeed is to always try to be better. If we accept that and realize just how important our soft skills are, we are well on our way to success in business and as a leader. Soft skills may be hard for some of us. That's okay. Where there is a will, there are ways to improve.

Being friendly and likable matters—it matters a lot.

Our mood is contagious. If we have a positive frame of mind and manner, it ignites a spirit of good energy, collaboration, trust, pride in our work, respect for our colleagues, and healthy risk-taking.

Our language, what we say, how we say it, our tone of voice, and how we show up and present ourselves to others influence their frame of mind and responsiveness to what we are communicating.

We need to understand our tendencies when under stress, frustrated, or angry. With this self-awareness, we can anticipate difficult situations and plan how we will respond—not react, respond—with conscious actions, words, and decisions.

Relationships truly matter. All too often, though, we may focus on client relationships, and not give enough attention to our internal relationships, except maybe our manager. If we ignore the feelings of our colleagues, we do not help morale. Quite the contrary.

Let's make our emotional intelligence a high priority, which will help our career, our leadership, and our satisfaction.

7

EMPATHY SETS THE TONE FOR OUR RELATIONSHIPS

While similar to our previous chapter about emotional intelligence, I chose to have empathy be a separate chapter as I would like to highlight its importance. Empathy is being aware of, and sensitive to, the feelings and experiences of others. This attentiveness makes our work more rewarding, effective, and pleasant, and it makes our company a better place.

While our responsibilities and titles differ, all of us in our company are colleagues. We all face challenges, be they personal or professional—often both. Recognizing that we are all trying to do the best we can despite perhaps unseen difficulties helps us appreciate that others struggle just as we do at times.

Our empathy is an energy that fuels those around us, our relationships, the spirit of our team, and our company. Culturally, empathy reinforces that we are a team in our work and in our support for one another. It communicates our concern for the well-being of others, not just their productivity.

Being empathic means being understanding and compassionate. Ideally, this is the way to live our lives. If we can slow down and show kindness with the gifts of our presence and attention to those with whom we work, we enhance the morale of our team and company. And what is more important than an excited, connected, positive team?

We are on this earth to care about and serve others. If we can help others—including when they are challenged, struggling, or needing comfort—we are making a difference in their lives. We don't do it for the recognition. We do it because we genuinely care about our colleagues. We sincerely want to help them succeed, and at times that means our being observant and offering our support and encouragement.

Empathy is how we show up and how we take the time to give our caring attention to listen carefully to others. When we speak, it is with a pleasant tone of voice. It is connecting with one another. It is wanting to help others and not being focused on our own personal benefit.

It takes commitment and time to earn trust in our relationships. We truly have to be interested in the other person and their well-being. It is our non-judgmental, approachable, and available disposition that allows others to be honest and vulnerable with their thoughts, feelings, challenges, and situation.

Regardless of our position, we can slow down, even if just a little, to have conversations with others in our company, checking in, reaching out to those who are quiet, withdrawn, or struggling. This is a mark of a great leader, one who cares about the collective whole and each individual part of it.

A note about emotions. We all get emotional at times. It is just a natural part of who we are. If we get upset, we can take a moment to pause, ask what happened, understand why we are feeling the way we are, and then compose ourselves so we can act respectfully and honestly.

Getting emotional at times shows that our work matters a great deal to us. This is a powerful message to our team members. If we show our passion about our work, likely we inspire others to do the same.

If someone breaks down under stress and cries, so what? She or he may be embarrassed, and yet I offer that there is no reason to be. Let's just accept that this happens at times—and still, let's go out and win the day.

Crying at work is not harmful; while losing our temper, maybe going into a rage with our words and actions, and hurting someone's feelings, is harmful.

If we share how we feel, we show who we really are. This has a powerful effect on others. It is how we create a culture of vulnerability, trust, and mutual respect, which provide a firm foundation for strong internal relationships.

Empathy and vulnerability help us be our very best as a teammate and a leader.

> *Empathy is one of our greatest tools in business*
> *that is most underused.*
>
> – Daniel Lubetzky, CEO of Kind

It is essential that we avoid office and company politics. It would be wishful thinking that internal politics do not exist. Unfortunately, there may always be some element of politics in a company, and maybe most likely in larger companies.

Still, we want to rise above these practices and attitudes and model being a good member of our team and company. We will be respected as such. This is what senior leaders want from their people.

I recently read a quote, which in essence said, "I enjoy my work, but I hate the internal politics."

Surely internal politics is a negativity, and negativity is a disease and only hurts the culture of our team and company. No one wants that and it only makes whoever is the cause of the negativity look bad.

If we see others "playing up" to the powers to be, talking behind people's backs, and/or seeking credit and the spotlight for themselves, we could speak with them privately and encourage them to avoid these practices, as they do not reflect well on them and are not in the best interest of their team or our company.

Our speaking directly and privately with the person is doing the right thing.

If the person is overly focused on herself, our chance of helping to change that may be slim. If we do try to help, let's be sure to state our positive intent upfront, that we want to be helpful, and that our conversation is in strict confidence. Maybe there is even a story we can share to illustrate the benefit of avoiding internal politics and competition, or perhaps there is a relevant article, TED Talk, or book we could recommend.

As mentioned, I had the benefit of working in a company for many years where we were all encouraging and supporting one another. We all believed that there was room at the top for people who were high performers, great teammates, and helped make things better.

We had a blast working together and helping one another. Competition was outside our company.

Actually, being a large company there were no doubt some elements of politics. That said, I do believe that where this "maneuvering" did exist, it was the lesser-performing and insecure people doing so. The best people were happy, believed in themselves, and trusted in our leaders and our culture.

Let's always try to be a positive influence on our teammates, our manager, and other colleagues to help us have a healthy organizational culture.

For example, we do not complain. If we see a problem, try to fix it or share our ideas for solution.

Be the light that is a source of good spirit and enthusiasm, that reinforces a "We can do it" attitude, that encourages collaboration and teamwork. This will be attractive to everyone in our company, and know that our senior executives want people who help make things better.

Enthusiasm and a positive attitude are contagious. People will respect our approach and values, and likely will want to model it themselves.

Catch people doing a good job, and thank them. Be genuine. No insincere platitudes, which people will sense.

Remember, everyone wants to feel that they are appreciated and valued. Let them know when they deserve it—people below us, above us, and our peers. It can help make their day, maybe their week, and will only lead to helping make things better.

As stated, this means avoiding office politics, and also absolutely, never talking poorly about others behind their backs.

We mention elsewhere the regional leader who so admired her colleague because he never spoke behind someone's back, not once in the eight years they have worked together. She knows this says a great deal about her colleague and his character, and why he will continue to advance in the company.

It saddens me that so often I hear someone talk negatively about someone else in the company. I understand it, and I certainly was guilty of that myself. When I think back, I wish I had not. It is a regret I carry with me.

Not liking someone, in general, is unhealthy for everyone: ourselves, the other person, and our company. Admittedly, there are times when it is justified. Yet, if we speak privately with the person, with a positive intent and open mind, and if we could truly get to know the other person, understand their story, and why they are like they are, that understanding may help shed our hostility.

Having healthy relationships helps us feel good and be in a wholesome mood, and we feel connected.

Our company's senior leadership will want people who have the courage to address their issues privately with another person.

In the modern version of the classic movie *Cinderella*, when her mother was on her deathbed and just before she passed, she shared with Cinderella this advice: "Have courage and be kind."

Good advice for all of us in business. It fosters our getting along.

John Fontana of Fontana Leadership Development and the Ignatian Legacy Fellows Program offers from his work that once someone knows another person's story, the understanding allows previous judgments to pass and may well lead to a genuine desire to like the other person. This is common in AA meetings; when people allow themselves to be vulnerable and share their stories, people gain an appreciation and fondness for one another. They are then rooting for and supporting each other.

It is in knowing and being known that appreciation of one another occurs.

If we harbor a dislike for a colleague, let's try to get to know the person, to understand her better. Maybe an unhurried conversation over coffee or a walk. Just maybe we'll find that our understanding will change how we feel about this person. This could be a win/win, and for the two of us maybe even to smile when we are together in the future.

Smiles are so good for the spirit of our people and our corporate culture. Happy people do better work. It is certainly worth our trying, and to encourage others to do likewise.

PepsiCo CEO Indra Nooyi says the best piece of career advice she ever received is "Assume positive intent."

Spiritual leaders offer that it helps to pray for someone we may have questions about, even dislike, as it helps change our disposition towards the person, opening our mind to a more positive, empathic attitude.

Let's do our very best to be a role model, to keep our minds open, to assume the best, to be empathic, to avoid judging others, and to bring positive energy, and only positive energy, with our smile, our warmth, our kindness, and our open mind.

We can model the change we want to see, be a team member who energizes our culture, and be the candle that lights the way for others.

8

STRIVING FOR IMPROVEMENT LEADS TO SUCCESS

A key success and leadership quality is to recognize that we can always be better and to strive for continuous improvement. Whether we are the CEO, a high-level executive, on our way up the corporate ladder, at the reception desk, or in the mailroom, everyone can improve.

This is a wonderful attitude to have ourselves, as it also is for a team and for our company or organization itself.

Wanting and working to be better flows from our humility—that we're good, maybe very good, and knowing that we can be even better.

When one has a big ego, does not seek advice, does not ask purposeful open-ended questions, does not listen to understand and learn, does not openly seek and want honest, timely, and constructive advice and feedback, that person will have limited success over time.

A team and a company that has a culture of "We're good, and we are going to try to get better every day" could well become the best in their field and their people will love working together.

Continuous improvement requires input from clients, such as:

- What does each client expect, want, and need from us? Each client may well be different. We must ask for specifics (e.g., what would that look like?).

- What advice do our co-workers have for us?

Seeking ideas and advice leads to a team that is engaged, excited, loyal, and eager for success, and they appreciate the great value of bottom-up ideas.

Keys to striving for continuous improvement are:

- Having the confidence to allow ourselves to be vulnerable.

- Knowing that we can always be better.

- Asking for ideas, advice, and feedback.

I had the good fortune of working with two organizations that were striving to become better every day. This was a real difference maker for each of us personally and for our companies.

Let's each initiate a plan or a campaign, or reinforce it if it already exists, to strive every day for improvement. This means seeking to help others in our company, and most definitely our manager, direct reports, and team members.

Make "How may I help you?" a routine, a part of our everyday life.

We need to make things happen—that is, to help make things better.

I mentioned that recently in a 360 Leadership Assessment I was told by the person's manager, "He has never asked how he may help me." The manager has a broad array of responsibilities and demands on his attention. He is disappointed that this team member would not want to pitch in beyond his own duties. He feels there is something lacking in the person's attitude, and this will limit his success and future with the company—and it is a great company, a leader in its field.

We must do excellent work, be selfless, be alert to and ask how we may help others, including our manager as well as our teammates and other colleagues. Likely, our leadership will be noticed and we will advance.

We do not have to be bold and outspoken to be a leader. Most of the effective leaders I have known and have even worked with are soft-spoken, kind, and thoughtful. Quiet leadership is very attractive.

An owner of a successful business, which continues to expand to new levels, told me that when she looks to promote someone, the particularly important qualities in her selection process are that the person truly wants to be successful herself and as a team, has "fire in her belly," is always looking to be helpful, and is an attentive and intentional listener.

She wants a person who is innovative, has an inherent desire to make things better for the company, and is also always looking to improve herself as well.

One person she has helped move up quickly personifies these qualities and is proactive in taking the initiative to help customers and clients and in problem-solving. She is a self-starter and does not wait to be told.

The owner also mentioned that this person has the quiet confidence to contribute her ideas and she works hard, will go the extra mile when needed, and is totally reliable. She can be counted on. In addition—and this is important—she has an engaging smile and a cheerful attitude. People know she enjoys her work and helping others.

By the way, this person is a single mom with a young son and does have boundaries about her availability, as first and foremost is her presence with her son when he is not at school. Also, she is an introvert. We will discuss the power of introverts in a later chapter.

The book, *The Zillion Dollar Coach*, is about Bill Campbell, an amazing leader, executive, and coach at companies like Google and Apple. When Bill would hire someone, the two key qualities to him were (1) honesty and (2) being coachable. There was no way he would select someone who was not forthright and honest, nor someone who was not open and eager to learn and grow—and continually learn and grow.

Campbell believed in not simply good communication, but excellent communication! He believed in walking the halls to be with and get to know our people. He encouraged regular conversations, and would often begin by asking what would be helpful to discuss. He was dead set against internal competition, rather to be a true team. He wanted his people to have courage, to speak up, to volunteer for the stretch and important assignments, and to help one another.

Being open and eager to be a lifelong learner fuels our effectiveness in business. We can all learn from each other, from our colleagues, as well as from outside resources.

Great leaders help assure goals are met. They coach their people, knowing that it is their people who achieve the results.

Mentoring is important, as is coaching. There is a difference. Mentoring is when a more experienced and generally more knowledgeable person shares how she achieved her success and offers advice to help a person's growth going forward.

Normally, a coach does not tell or advise someone; she asks purposeful questions to help the person draw out from within herself what she could do to achieve her desired outcomes. The coach believes that each person is creative, resourceful, and whole. Many people just need help in determining the right things for them to do to enhance their effectiveness. That does not mean they have any less potential, they just may benefit from help from someone who cares, and who helps them seek the wisdom within themselves.

Many who benefit significantly from coaching are already doing a great job and are successful. They treasure having someone to ask them purposeful questions, someone they may speak with in total confidence as they know the conversations are confidential, maybe someone who will challenge them, discuss best practices, be their thinking partner, and other benefits that may help them improve even more.

Other people who could gain from coaching are those who are not asking questions and asking for help, as they view that as a weakness (it is a strength), may be in the wrong job, do not trust others, look to blame others, may not be open to feedback, lack self-awareness, can be defensive and/or close-minded, and a myriad of similar characteristics.

However, if the person is not open to learn and grow, coaching will likely not be effective.

I know the potential benefits one can receive. I personally had a coach when I was a senior executive with important leadership responsibilities. My coach, Mary Mavis, helped me with my being conflict-avoidant.

I am so thankful for Mary, as it was vitally important that I learned how to have the difficult conversations, address the elephant in the room, to try to help a difficult person, and if the person's attitude did not change, we had to move that person off the bus.

A coach will ask about a person's goals and desired outcomes and ask what she thinks she needs to do, and why, to achieve these outcomes. There may well be options to weigh for her to choose the best approach.

It takes humility and quiet confidence to be coachable.

Coachable people seek out those who speak truth to them, even if it is a painful truth, because it protects them and it makes them a better person and leader.

– Gary Rohrmayer

In addition to perhaps investing in a coaching relationship, I encourage reading an insightful leadership book every month, if possible, and to have a network of people we admire for their character, judgment, and accomplishments with whom we may discuss ideas and issues.

If we are eagerly seeking to grow, and are coachable, we will be noticed and appreciated.

9

QUESTIONS ARE OUR
BEST FRIENDS

It is so important to know what success looks like in virtually everything we do at work for our company and for clients. It begins with our manager. What does she expect and want from me? And we need details and clarity, so we may focus on delivering just that.

If we have a drive to succeed and we realize that we need clarity of what is expected and needed from us, hopefully that will lead us to ask our manager and/or our teammates and others questions such as:

- What do you need and what from me?
- By when?
- Would you like me to check in with you? When?
- What would you like the final result to look like?
- How will you know that you are fully satisfied?
- What advice do you have for me?
- What have I not asked?

I cannot overemphasize the importance of clarity. It gives us the picture of success so we may focus on delivering specifically what is needed and wanted. Ideally our questions are open-ended, that is, beginning with:

- What
- How
- Why
- Who
- When
- Where

The What, How, and Why are most important. They are our mainstays.

We have a right to ask these questions to gain clarity. If we are hesitant, I encourage mustering up the courage. If we need to explain, it is fine to say we want to do a great job and want a picture of success so we may strive to deliver exactly that.

"Why" helps us understand what our work means. That can be exhilarating and help inspire our desire to do an excellent job and to help our colleagues do so as well.

Asking questions is how we learn. In fact, people I especially admire in business, in the academic world, and clergy in the church are those who ask questions and want to continue to learn. Peter Hill, the CEO of Billy Casper Golf, the leader in the golf course management field, is the classic example of a lifelong learner. Peter believes that he only learns when he is listening, not when he is speaking, and he asks purposeful questions. He is one of the most respected leaders in the golf industry, with good reason.

I have known Peter for nearly 40 years. He has always been a learner, has always asked purposeful questions.

My wife, Kerry, and I speak frequently with three young dynamic priests in the Chicago area, Fr. Max Behna, Fr. Matt Litak, and Fr. Tim Anastos. Each has humility and is committed to continue to learn and grow, to be the very best they can be in serving others. They ask questions, they listen attentively, reflect back what they hear, and they take notes.

We should all be this way. This is how we continue to improve. The principle of striving for continuous improvement as the path to success is repeated throughout this book. Rightfully so.

Among our very most important questions would be to ask our manager, our teammates and other colleagues, and those who report to us such questions as:

- What specifically do you feel I could do better?
- How could I be more effective and more helpful?
- What advice do you have for me?

Be sure to explain upfront that we would appreciate honest answers, as we want to be effective as a teammate and the best version of ourselves. In doing so we will gain a wealth of valuable ideas.

Asking these questions requires our allowing ourselves to be vulnerable and recognizing that we have areas of potential improvement, things we can do better. Everyone does.

Discussing our areas of potential improvement with others helps us make these changes and to have a more rewarding work environment. Discussion is the fuel of change and connection.

There is also the practice of asking ourselves questions, and being honest about reality—reality as it is, not reality as we hope it is. David Emerald wrote *The Power of TED*: *The Empowerment Dynamic*, a worthy read about creating the result we want, rather than being stuck in the victim mode. David has a new book, *3 Vital Questions*. He offers that we regularly ask our self:

- Where is my focus?

- How are my relationships?

- What steps/actions am I taking?

This is simple and helpful. It focuses us on the right outcomes (our desired outcomes), developing and maintaining solid relationships founded on respect and trust while taking action, even baby steps, toward our goals, which gives us a positive mindset.

Asking questions is the fuel for growth, saves time, and ensures success, connection, and trust with our clients and colleagues. It is a most valuable tool for us.

PRINCIPLES THAT SERVE US WELL AND LEAD TO SUCCESS

- Whatever our field, we are in a people business, and our relationships matter greatly; our co-workers are our internal clients.

- Catch people doing a good job.

- Happy employees do better work.

- Walk the halls or pick up the phone, lead with humility and empathy, connect with our people, and ask how they are doing and how we may help.

10

LISTEN, LISTEN, AND THEN LISTEN

Listen to understand and learn.

Working with a great many highly successful executives, I've learned that for all their business acumen, the key to their effectiveness is their ability to listen attentively to their people. The most effective leaders make the time to meet face to face when possible; or when not, to pick up the phone. This is a difference-maker.

In the coaching world, it is offered that listening is our gift to someone. So true. Intentional listening is a gift of our respect to others and builds trust. As team members and leaders, it is also our responsibility.

We must recognize that while many of us may think we are good listeners, most of us actually are not.

Comments I often hear are:

- "He does not seem to be fully present in our conversations; he is distracted."
- "He may think he is listening, but does he really hear the meaning of what is being said?"
- "He is listening, but is he really hearing?"

- "He talks at me, not with me."

Attentive listening does not come naturally to most of us. Our ability to retain what we hear is substantially limited. Surveys reveal that we generally remember less than 50 percent, and perhaps as little as 20 percent, of what we hear. A *Harvard Business Review* article cites research indicating that within 48 hours, we may retain only 25 percent of what we've heard.

No matter how effective (or ineffective) we are at listening, we can all improve, and we should all make improvement a priority.

Women tend to be better at purposeful listening. They notice dynamics and are skillful with conversation. Women's and men's brains are wired differently, so women may notice what men often do not.

As most women are good listeners and communicators, we would be well advised to learn from them, as well as having more women in leadership positions.

If there were more women in senior leadership, we would hear less about the "we versus they" dynamic; for example, middle management versus senior management, and the field versus home office. Women, in general, tend to value relationships and care about their entire team.

Let's encourage women to step up and help our companies become listening companies—companies that listen attentively not only to our clients but also to our own people. This would be an important transformation as attentive, conscious listening makes an important and positive difference in our organizational culture.

Here's a story that illustrates why we need women in important positions. A company had been trying to gain a new client, an especially desirable client. They had been working with the prospect for ten months, but just could not get a favorable decision. They were stuck, and felt they had done everything they could. Finally, one of their senior executives, a woman, asked to review their work, including learning about the people on the buyer's side. When she asked her sales team what was preventing the deal, they responded that the female executive hadn't been convinced. It became clear that the sales team, who were all men, had focused their attention on the prospect's senior male executives. When the sales team was asked, "What is the female executive's name?" the men on the sales team all hung their heads, as none of them knew her name, nor had there been any communication with her.

The men heard that the female executive had concerns about the partnership, yet they were not fully listening as they never invited her into their discussions. It took a woman executive from their own company to teach them the value of appreciating everyone, listening behind the words, and inviting all those necessary to the table for discussion.

When we do listen attentively, consciously, intentionally, purposefully, or actively—which are all terms used for effective listening—we not only learn ourselves, we also honor the other person.

A CEO I know exemplifies this idea beautifully. He was recruited to lead a very successful organization that was struggling for the first time in its long existence. He very capably brought this company back. At his retirement, his co-workers each wrote personal notes, which reflected the way he led by listening:

- "You listened to everyone's suggestions, ideas, and goals."
- "You helped mold us into a real team."
- "You gave each one of us increased dignity by listening and by caring."
- "Your faith in us lifted the spirits of everyone here."

- "Your calm leadership and belief in each person's importance and potential empowered us all."

If we are listening attentively, our team members, clients, and service providers feel valued, which is so important to our success as a team member, a leader, and to our company.

Everyone wants to feel appreciated, valued, and heard, and that their ideas matter.

Business is about relationships. It is imperative that we connect with people—that is, our external and our internal clients, our team members. We do this by truly listening to them.

Listening to understand and learn is the way to connect and to bond with others. It conveys respect and builds trust and rapport.

One CFO told me that when she senses her CEO is only half listening, as he seems to have some of his attention on his computer monitor or smart phone, she'll ask him, "Should I come back at another time when you can be fully focused on our conversation?"

Good for her to address this, as she should. Most people might be hesitant to speak up in this way with their boss. We should speak up, though.

A former colleague told me that at her new company, the COO was somewhat isolated from those not in the executive wing. She was in line to become the next President, though most people were less than enthusiastic about that as they felt she did not really know them, nor they her. She carried two cell phones with her, and was constantly instant messaging.

She had a 360 Leadership Assessment and was taken back by learning that her colleagues felt she was "standoffish." She has taken this to heart. She now tries to have meetings outside her office, maintains eye contact during conversations, and listens attentively. Her colleagues have her full attention now, as she is not distracted. They are getting more done and are more efficient, and mutual respect abounds.

Yes, listening is so very important, and it is not easy to do patiently with all the busyness and demands on our time. It definitely requires our full attention, and our patience and practice.

As with so many things, attentive listening is founded on our attitude. We must want to listen to understand and learn. Our attitude and commitment help so much.

Each time I have facilitated in-house workshops, presented webinars, and written short articles on improving listening skills, I have always received appreciative feedback. People are grateful for the ideas offered and realize their need to improve their listening skills.

To illustrate just how much attentive listening means, I always bear in mind what my amazing friend and coaching colleague, Carylynn Larson, PhD, says: *"Being heard is like being loved. It is hard to describe, but you know it when you feel it."*

People we work with need to feel we care about them. If we really listen attentively, they will know we do care.

Fortunately, listening, like all other skills, can be improved. With specific self-observation practices, we all can improve our listening.

There are many excellent books that can help us improve our listening. One of them is John Maxwell's *Everyone Communicates, Few Connect.* This title is perfect: it is true and so important to realize.

We must make the time to connect with our team members and other This means walking the halls or picking up our phone and having conversations.

Once we start a conversation, we must consciously listen with a quiet mind and without an agenda. In this way, we are offering space to build mutual understanding. When we approach conversations with an open mind, we encourage growth, both ours and that of the person with whom we are speaking.

When we are in conversation, let's try to slow down and not be in a rush. Let's not check our phones. Instead, let's enter the conversation fully. Otherwise, if we are impatient or talk briskly, then, as Maxwell insightfully observes, *"People may hear our words, but they feel our attitude."*

Active listening is having a clear mind, not judging the person, and while the speaker is talking not thinking about whether we agree or what we are going to say. It requires that we quiet our mind, which is not easy. We need to let our thoughts subside, perhaps even picturing them floating out of our heads as if they are clouds.

Most of us listen with a problem-solving mind, "Oh, I know what she should do." We are not truly focused, or maybe we are focused on ourselves and what we think, rather than on what the speaker is saying to us.

We must be intentional. We must fully focus on the other person and listen with comfortable eye contact, offering affirmations so she knows we are listening and that we care. Let's turn away from distractions and pay close attention. If we take brief notes during or after conversations, we show that we are listening and that we do care.

When in conversation, use silence to allow the person to think and maybe continue with their thoughts. The silence also allows us to think about what we have heard, and hopefully to understand the other person's reasoning and feelings.

The use of silence is a key ingredient of intentional listening. We should always listen more than we speak. A guideline that we could follow is the 80/20 rule, listening 80 percent of the time and speaking only 20 percent.

There is an insightful principle, *"Let silence do the heavy lifting."*

To summarize, here are key points to becoming a better listener:

- Decide that we want to be an intentional and better listener. By making this conscious decision, we are more aware of when we are truly listening and when our mind is wandering.
- Quiet our mind.
- Let our thoughts float out of our head as if they are clouds.
- Although difficult, make every effort to suspend assessing, judging, and problem-solving.
- Do not think about what we will say.
- Focus on what the other person is saying and not saying, and sense what they may be feeling.
- Pay attention to their tone of voice, body language, and other nonverbal cues.
- Use silence.
- Listen 80 percent of the time.
- Lean in towards the person, maintain comfortable eye contact, smile and nod when appropriate. This signals affirmation and that we are listening to understand.
- Ask clarifying and follow-up questions about what is being said, which demonstrate we care.

The best way to practice listening is to enter into conversations in business during the week, and with family and friends on weekends, with the intent of listening with a quiet mind, focused solely on the other person, not on our own thoughts. After a conversation, take a minute or two to observe how we did. Did we listen effectively? How did we feel? Were we calm and patient, and did we have an open mind? How did the other person seem to feel? How were we received? What effect did our listening have?

We can tell when we've listened well and when we could have been better.

These self-observation practices definitely help improve the quality of our listening.

Numerous clients have selected improved listening skills as a desired outcome of our coaching relationship, and they seem pleased as their relationships with those with whom they work improve and they feel that they themselves are more effective leaders as a result.

I recommend *Active Listening: Improve Your Ability to Listen and Lead.* This is a 32-page guidebook with a wealth of information about listening skills that will help each of us. It is available from the Center for Creative Leadership, www.ccl.org.

Nearly every great leader I have worked with has told me that they consider listening to be their most important skill.

11

CHARACTER: THE FOUNDATION OF OUR SUCCESS

Our character signals so much about our business and leadership potential. If we are grounded with strong character, have sound values, discipline, and a desire to serve others, then we can be highly effective and respected.

From our character flow our thoughts, words, decisions, actions, attitude, and an earnest desire to be of service and helpful to others.

Integrity is the foundation of good character. It means doing the right things, even when no one is looking. It means making decisions that are best for our team members and for our company, not for our own convenience or benefit. It means being an upstanding person who is quick to share credit.

It takes strong character to accept responsibility when things do not go well, rather than looking to blame someone else. When we do take ownership, our honesty, humility, and inner confidence make us more human and trustworthy.

Integrity, honesty, humility, and inner confidence shape our moral compass and provide a foundation for dealing with challenging situations, as well as helping us bring out the best in others.

We must always strive to do the right thing—that which is ethical. At times, this means we may not be popular. We do the right thing because we know that in the end, it is what is proper. We follow our instincts.

To lead with integrity we must "say what we mean and mean what we say." There is no room for deception. And we need to deliver what we promise.

Discipline and self-management give us the fortitude to do the hard things and to respectfully share what we think. The demands on us and our time are great. We have to use our time as an investment, and not be at the mercy of the clock.

- Do our colleagues know that we value them?
- Do we have one-on-one conversations with them?
- Do we treat them with encouragement, respect, and dignity?

Let's develop our awareness of the human side of our company. How do we do that? We develop our emotional intelligence skills, our:

- Self-awareness
- Awareness of the feelings of others
- Self-management
- Relationship management

This is key to our character and can be learned and improved. We can assess our current skill levels in these areas and commit to become better.

These emotional intelligence qualities allow us to respond with poise, not react, to our people. They help us understand the various dynamics that occur among our teammates, and allow us to act with composure in ways that are respectful and honoring of all.

These skills are key indicators of success in business as a teammate and a leader.

Our attitude is infectious. We must speak only positively about people to others. If we have a problem or a difficult message for a person, we must have the courage to come out from behind ourselves and speak directly with that person, in private. If we degrade or talk behind someone's back, it's we who lose the respect of others, and it taints our character.

Let's ask ourselves:

- Who am I right now?
- Am I being as effective as I could be?
- Where did I fall short today?
- How can I do things/act differently the next time to be more congruent with who I want to be?
- What specific steps can I take to improve?
- Whom can I share my personal development goals with?
- Who will give me ongoing feedback that is truthful and insightful so that I can strive to be the best version of myself?

While the previous chapter is specifically about listening, I wish to reiterate its importance. One giant step we can all take is to become a better listener, an attentive listener, someone who has learned to quiet her mind, to not think about solutions while listening, and not make judgments, but rather to be simply focused on what the speaker is saying—and is not saying, which can be revealing. And it is being aware of the speaker's emotions—again, this can also be revealing.

Isn't it strange that we are seldom taught listening skills? Attentive listening is work. It takes conscious practice to quiet our mind while listening, and try to stay absolutely focused, quiet, tuned in, and aware of the emotions present. It is not easy, as many of us naturally have problem-solving minds.

An approach to thinking about character is to think about what it means to be a lady or a gentleman. These are some of the qualities of ladies and gentlemen:

- Thoughtfulness
- Carrying oneself with quiet dignity
- Good manners toward all
- Integrity
- Humility
- Quiet confidence
- Respectful
- Genuine care for others
- Considering others' needs before our own

Ladies and gentlemen also tend to be good communicators, especially by:

- Listening with open minds
- Asking important questions
- Listening a lot more than we speak

I remember well my days years ago at Georgetown University, when every day the Jesuits spoke with us about being "Ladies and Gentlemen of Georgetown." The messages were that as ladies and gentlemen, we were to carry ourselves with grace and humility, to do what is right, and that we are meant to serve others. This is why we are here on earth.

Grace is how we interact with and treat others with genuine care and dignity.

Recently, a friend and I had a conversation about the way colleagues treat one another. We lamented the fact that some people speak negatively about others behind their backs. She said she tries never to do that, as she believes there is a place for grace in business.

What a wonderful principle to reflect upon.

The dictionary defines grace as "a controlled, polite, and pleasant way of behaving." For me, grace is conveyed by the way we think, act, and carry ourselves. It's how we are with other people. It's believing in the good in others and helping cultivate and draw that goodwill and kindness out.

We certainly want others in our company to embody grace in their everyday work.

Grace is having the strength of character to speak directly and privately with a person we have a problem with, in a polite and helpful manner.

Grace is being encouraging. It is asking how we can help. It is complimenting others on their work, helping them to feel good about themselves.

Being that source of positive energy that lifts the spirits of our team members and other colleagues is grace, as when someone is struggling, carrying a heavy load of stress, worry, or grief due to personal or family issues, and we show we care, that we are there to listen, and maybe even pray with the person.

I consider Bill Dunn, a senior leader at Johnson & Higgins, to be one of my finest mentors. Bill was always composed, with a soft smile, always ready to quietly help others succeed. He was also a doer. Outside of J&H, he was mayor of his village, a member of the vestry of his church, and actively helped numerous charitable organizations. We had a happy and proud team at J&H, thanks to Bill's leadership.

Colette Kleitz, formerly my colleague at the Damon Runyon Cancer Research Foundation, very ably headed development for the foundation. Colette was an ideal teammate—responsible, reliable, quietly cheerful, and quick to appreciate the good work of others. She helped others feel good about themselves. Colette presented herself with and radiated positive energy at all times. She raised our spirits with her grace.

Grace is in our soft skills, our being a caring person, treating others with respect and dignity.

People appreciate being treated with grace. We ourselves also benefit greatly from establishing a culture of graciousness. We will be more at ease and present, and will reflect a peace of mind and gratitude.

Business is about relationships. Isn't all of life about relationships? Life is not a solitary event. Our families, friends, and colleagues are all around us. When we develop and maintain these relationships with genuine care, honesty, and trust, with no hidden agenda, we invite meaningful engagement, respect, and trust.

This is grace in action.

I believe in hiring good people, being clear about expectations and goals, assuring that they have what they need to succeed, and then under-managing—letting them do great work without bureaucratic control. When we show appreciation and respect, our people work hard to live up to our level of trust in them. They strive to do their very best because they feel appreciated, valued, and heard, and that they are an important member of our team.

When we take a few moments to greet everyone warmly and to ask how their day is going, and listen patiently with genuine interest, we are improving relationships. We show that we appreciate them, and that goes a long way to inspiring a strong and winning culture.

Grace is humility coupled with quiet confidence and increases the positive influence we bring. It reflects our sound character.

PRINCIPLES THAT SERVE US WELL AND
LEAD TO SUCCESS

- Leaders are signal senders. What signals do we wish to *send?*

- Our emotions are contagious—and kindness is motivating.

- Avoid company politics and talking behind someone's back.

- Manage our time, and always try to be early.

12

BOOSTING OUR INNER CONFIDENCE

Confidence comes from improving.

I mentioned that I am writing this book as a number of people I think highly of seem to be stuck within their companies and careers. Please don't get me wrong: I in no way feel that our level of success in business defines who we are as a person. Not at all.

However, these people are intelligent, hardworking, dutiful, and are not self-serving. They are worthy of advancing to higher levels in their careers. What is missing? While each situation is different, the likely common element is low confidence.

Lower levels of confidence lead one to not speak up, not contribute her ideas, not volunteer, not build a network, not make things happen, and to avoid risk.

Yet I know these people have great potential and so much to offer their companies. If only they could summon the courage to step up and pursue making things better within their companies, they could be strong and successful leaders.

Having courage is easier said than done; however, it can be called upon when needed.

Just as an introvert is nearly always an introvert all of her life, she can control this. She knows how to commit to her job or company by managing her energy and tendency to avoid crowds, as she knows it is important to extend herself and have the necessary conversations.

We must manage our somewhat low level of confidence in like manner, calling upon our courage and speaking up and acting to do the right things, to help make things better.

There are many resources available to help us. If we want to advance to our level of potential, I encourage accessing them.

It is important that we:

- Contribute our ideas.
- Identify potential improvements.
- Always try to make good things happen and make things better.

I believe virtually everyone reading this book could help make things better in their company. We can all be alert to how to improve productivity, save time, streamline work, maybe a new product or service, grow our business, and maybe identify a potential new client.

What stops some from contributing these ideas is the notion that "that is not my job" and/or our hesitancy to take risk.

Everyone's job is to help make their company better.

We may not be personally able to land a new client, but if we see a company that might need what our company offers, there may be co-workers we can introduce to help make that happen.

It helps for each of us to bear in mind our "why."

What is our purpose in our work? Do we believe our purpose and desired outcome are to contribute to a winning team, to do our part to help our team, company, and those with whom we work to be better?

If yes, then a boost of our courage can enable us to think of the "higher ground" and speak up, to contribute our ideas, and to do what we feel is the right thing to do. If our intent is honorable, to be helpful, then let's not worry. Let's take two or three slow, deep breaths and exhale, think of our desired outcome (to be helpful), and do it—with our head held high.

Let's stay alert for potential improvements. See something that can be perfected or fixed, do so, or bring it to the attention of the right person (our manager or whomever).

And I say speak up, not simply send an email. I recommend speaking directly to our manager or whoever is the right person, and also giving that person our idea in writing and why it may be important (e.g., it could save our company money or have other potential benefits). I recommend an email in addition to the conversation, as some managers themselves may lack the confidence to present to their "higher ups." They will be less likely to sit on our idea and the "why" if they are in writing.

Those who are successful in business and in their companies tend to be those who are "doers." They don't wait to be told. They see an opportunity to make things better, to fix a problem, to help a colleague, and they act.

They are "go-getters." Well, really they are "go-givers."

The Nike creed "Just do it" is a good description of the mindset. Someone who does not let grass grow under her feet. She acts on her instincts, and is always looking for opportunities to:

- Help others
- Help our company grow
- Improve things
- Reduce our expenses and cost of doing business
- Save us time

As I mentioned in the introduction, I see really fine, capable people stand by and only do what they are told and is "their job." No, let's go out of our way to help our co-workers, our manager, everyone within our company— to help our company.

Be alert for opportunities to make things better. This is what leaders do, make things better.

This is also what a great teammate does—and remember, we are all team members, from our CEO to our receptionist and those in our mailroom. Anyone can spot an opportunity to do the right things, things that help.

This includes initiating the conversations that could have real potential for a positive impact. And it may well include conversation(s) we are avoiding, which could lead to fixing a problem or improving a situation with a difficult person.

If we want to get ahead, to maximize our potential, we cannot just be a spectator. We need to step up and do what may help make things and/or people better. Being naturally confident helps us do that. However, we can "manage" ourselves if we are hesitant, recognizing how we are feeling and that if we fail, we are not a failure. Everyone in our company has failed.

Almost certainly, we will be more respected for trying than for not acting, for staying on the sidelines.

Boosting our confidence level is a particularly important topic, as a great many of us are being held back by our negative and self-limiting talk, when in fact we have potential to make major contributions, advance to important roles, and be a highly effective leader.

Having the humility to accept and share that we always want to be trying to improve, and our having the quiet confidence to step up and out to share our ideas and to take on new and/or important work will definitely help our contributions to our company and the people of our company.

Men's generally high level of confidence can be an advantage; and at times it can also be dangerous, as with snap decisions or taking risk without discerning how it may affect others if it does not work out.

Women's generally lower level of confidence can be limiting. Fortunately, there is more and more support to help women lean in, step up, and realize they have so very much to contribute.

Women are more risk aware than men—not risk avoidant, risk aware—which is important. Risk awareness is needed!

We need women in senior and mid-level leadership positions. Simply put, companies and organizations should not be run by men only or predominantly men. We need more than one or two women in important positions so that they are heard, not dismissed or talked over.

I implore all women, as well as men, to believe in themselves. I know how much they could offer their companies. A confidence boost would make their leadership and contributions even greater, and their advancement would improve the results of their companies.

Marisa Peacock, founder of The Strategic Peacock, which helps organizations create and implement online marketing strategies, offers that it is important to understand why women often have lower confidence. It is not inherent; it is learned behavior. Historically, when women were not given opportunities, when they saw less qualified men in positions of power, when they were not encouraged to be assertive, their confidence level lessened their readiness to speak up and volunteer.

Many women who have low confidence are not born that way. It is often because of the male-dominated environments in business, religious organizations, and even family that can cultivate that deportment.

We must absolutely realize that those with a lower confidence level may well have every bit as much potential as those who do embody confidence.

When we are hesitant to do something or speak up, it is helpful to recognize what we are feeling. For example, are we afraid of failing? While it is easy to say we all have failed, it does take courage for some to take risk.

Failures are a door to go through to succeed.

As with so many goals and aspirations, we can begin to move ahead with small actions and mindsets. We can definitely feel better about ourselves with these simple actions:

- Be organized.
- Be prepared.
- Call people by their name.
- Take a genuine interest in others.
- Encourage and help others.
- Smile, and keep comfortable eye contact.
- Ask good questions.

- Listen to understand and learn.

- Get others to talk about themselves.

- Be well groomed, dressing neatly—for success.

- Always be 15 minutes early.

- Stand tall and walk purposefully.

- Exercise.

- Eat well.

- Get adequate rest.

- Assure that our spirituality is a priority.

- Stay in touch with family and friends, including old friends

- Be kindhearted.

- Be grateful.

- Contribute to our communities.

- Be in a positive frame of mind and a source of positive thinking and energy.

- Think about our desired outcome, the "higher ground," and take action and move forward, even beginning with baby steps.

These may seem like the basics, and they are. Yet often progress towards what we want to achieve flows from the basics, even baby steps. Baby steps change our mindset, as we are moving forward.

If we acknowledge that women generally, and some men, have a lower level of self-confidence, and accept the premise that a problem discussed is a problem half-solved, we can certainly be part of the solution. We can get together for conversations, ask how we can help one another, and be supportive and encouraging.

It is amazing how "Hey, you are good at that, nice work" is a boost to one's confidence. The more we encourage and help one another, women and men, gain self-confidence, the stronger our cultures and the better the financial results of our companies.

Cathy Becker, an astute and caring former colleague, says that "Leadership is how we help others feel about themselves." This is an insightful description and a good message for us to keep in mind within our everyday work. We can help lift up our colleagues.

Rebecca Johnson, PT, MPT, OCS, CMPT, CFMT, is the founder of TLAR Physical Therapy and an exceptional natural leader. I asked Rebecca about her thoughts on our inner confidence and how we may help ourselves. Here is what Rebecca shared:

Empowerment comes from someone who believes in us. It is more nurture than nature. Emulating confident and compassionate people in position of leadership will grow the seed in us.

Boosting confidence = Empowerment through many areas of our life:

- Knowledge and preparedness Builds Confidence.
- Feeling empowered, dressing for the position you want, Builds Confidence.
- Doing the right thing when faced with adversity Builds Confidence.
- Being a life-learner in all areas of our life—home, children, cooking, spirituality, fashion, relationships, leadership—Builds Confidence.
- Reflecting on what we do well Builds Confidence.
- Goal-setting Builds Confidence.
- Time management Builds Confidence.

- Seeking a mentor and/or a coach who we admire and who helps us realize our potential if we trust our abilities will Build Confidence.

- Surrounding our self with a great FAN Club (friends, teammates, relatives) that supports our passions and us as a person Builds Confidence.

- Being a reflection of who we want to be Builds Confidence.

Listen only to our positive, loving self-talk, and bid goodbye forever to our old self-limiting self-talk.

I recently listened to a webinar by Tara Mohr, coach and author of *Playing Big: Find Your Voice, Your Mission, Your Message*. She interviewed a number of successful leaders, all women, though the messages will also hold true for men. She asked what enhanced their career success? The top answers were greater confidence and finding a great mentor.

Tara offers that courage is a key, to trust our abilities and believe in ourselves, to speak up, raise our hand for stretch jobs, to take action in the midst of self-doubt, believing that we will likely succeed.

It is important to identify and name our inner critic, our self-talk, recognizing it as such and listening to a new voice that knows our capabilities and is ready for the challenges we encounter as we move up.

Let's not worry about pleasing others. Let's just do our best, and then we will be comfortable with ourselves and our contributions.

Lauree Ostrofsky, another amazing coach, and the author of *I'm Scared and Doing It Anyway*, recommends a simple approach to facing fear and stress, using actions such as:

- Take slow, deep breaths, drink water, wash our hands often.

- Brush our teeth while looking in the mirror and seeing ourselves and knowing we are loved and are special.

- Let people know we care about them; call them, write letters, smile at people as we pass them.

- Write in our gratitude journal.

- And my favorite: Make lemonade, which will give us our joyous smile, and with it, a confidence boost.

These thoughts, actions, and principles will help boost confidence and help foster important contributions. In fact, they will help a lot.

It is important that we speak up and offer our ideas. It may mean that we may have to learn to be comfortable being uncomfortable, and that we are comfortable being visible. This is often what it takes to advance, and if we do want to advance in our company, let's believe in ourselves.

A theme throughout this book is that leaders help make things (and people) better, and the same should be true of all of us. We all can be leaders.

We want to be a great team member, and contribute ideas to help grow our company, reduce expenses, improve morale and culture, help others grow, and do excellent work. Hopefully our company and our manager are encouraging us to contribute ideas. I say "hopefully," as I know that this is not always the case. Nevertheless, let's trust the process, that whatever our role, we should be thinking of how we ourselves, our team, and our company might improve.

Let's learn how to manage our inner voice that is holding us back and limiting us. Having a critical inner voice does not mean we are any less capable than those who have confidence and may act boldly. Not at all. I can think of a good number of friends and others who have some degree of a low self-image of themselves and yet are extremely gifted and talented. It is difficult for them to speak up, sometimes even when asked.

That said, if we want to get ahead in our company, we have to overcome our hesitancy.

One friend, with a strong financial background, working with a large company, understood that the president was not providing the leadership needed and the company's results were disappointing. He decided to step up and have the tough conversation with the president. Knowing the president was a football fan, my friend presented an analogy in football terms: if his football team had a number of consecutive poor seasons, it simply was time for a change, that is, a new coach. He was not critical of the president, but simply offered that a change could be helpful. The president did retire and the company began to do better, as did my friend's career.

While this may be an extreme example, my friend told me what allowed him to have that difficult conversation with his president was his faith, that he trusted God, and that he knew it was the right thing to do.

Certainly more common examples are contributing ideas in meetings and in conversations. It is important that we offer our thoughts—honest thoughts—respectfully.

I feel very strongly about this, and I pray for those who read this book to please realize the importance of contributing our ideas, and encouraging our colleagues to do so as well. Certainly, ideas must be contributed in a respectful way, so everyone knows that our purpose is to be helpful and that we are not motivated by self-interest. State our positive intention up front.

Speaking up definitely can be difficult. Again, done respectfully, it should nearly always be appreciated and admired. I can think of a number of times when I struggled, and sometimes did not say what I wanted to. This was my bad. I failed to do the right thing.

For some, speaking up is relatively easy, but for others it is not. It takes courage, at times even for those who are generally confident. Yet to move ahead in business and reach our potential, we must learn to have courage, take risk, speak up, and always try to make things better.

I should offer a word of caution, as illustrated in this story. Someone I especially admire as an outstanding professional and servant leader would at times respectfully offer her ideas; and her manager, who was insecure, could not accept someone would had opinions that did not agree with his own, so he eliminated her position. This was an exception, and I suspect they did not have a good working relationship to begin with.

*She now has a better job, with a better company, and greater career advance-*ment opportunities, and she is happier.

We must follow our instinct about when and how to speak up, and just know that it is generally, nearly always, the right thing to do.

13

COMMUNICATE WELL
AND OFTEN

*Communication is your ticket to success, if we pay
attention and to do it effectively.*

– Theo Gold

Our communication is key to success in business, as in our relationships and in life. In fact, most problems, big and small, could be solved with honest communication, both being open and truthful in expressing ourselves and in our attentive listening to learn and understand.

Constructive working relationships are aided by understanding what good communication looks like between two people. This must be discussed and clarified by the parties. Each of us is different, and we cannot assume that what is good communication to one person is the same for another person.

One leader told me she was heading a large department in a financial services company and had seven people reporting to her. She wanted each of the seven to let her know every Monday morning how things went the previous week and what were the priorities for this week. She was surprised at the range of communication preferences. One team leader wanted to give her a brief written summary. Another team leader also wanted to give her a written summary, all bullet points for the highlights and only with additional written content as needed. Another team leader asked if she could meet with her for 15 or so minutes each Monday. Yet another, a particularly quick thinking and acting and highly effective team leader, wanted to stand at her door early each Monday and quickly report about activities and accomplishments the prior week and their primary issues and plans for this week, and to answer questions and receive advice she may have.

What a variety. Yet, each communication plan worked effectively. As a leader, she wants to meet each person where they are. Her team leaders appreciated that, and they have a smooth running and high-performing department.

Whatever our position, be it high-level or mid-level management—actually wherever we are in our company, we want to communicate openly and regularly with those to whom we report, with our peers, those who may report to us, and with other colleagues.

We do not need to have long conversations. There is an Irish proverb, "Say a little and say it well."

Nearly every leader I've spoken with in writing this book say they particularly admire and will try to help advance those who do excellent work, have leadership qualities themselves, are great teammates, are humble and eager to learn and grow—and absolutely that they are good communicators. Good communication is essential.

The path to developing and maintaining high-quality relationships is conversations, one-on-one conversations. It is how people know we care about them—and people certainly want to know we care.

Conversations must be two-way, and we should listen a good bit more than we speak. We must be fully present, not looking at our smart phone or computer, not thinking about what we will say, not making judgments.

Put people at ease, perhaps smile, if appropriate, comfortable eye contact, using the person's name, giving affirmations, using reflective listening, asking clarifying questions, listening to understand and learn. We want the person to feel heard and understood.

Of course, there are numerous options for our communications, including conversations in person or by phone, Skype, FaceTime or Zoom, email, texts, and letters or hand-written notes. In general, I believe texts should be used for the most timely and important messages. Many may receive literally hundreds of emails each day, and so our email messages may be watered down in importance. This is something we should work out with each person individually.

I am a believer in stopping by to see someone in person or at least picking up the phone. It happens too infrequently these days. One CEO told me she had about two hours in an airport before her plane boarded. She pulled out her laptop to be in touch by email with two former clients and two prospects. Just before she sent the first email, she remembered a discussion about the power of picking up the phone versus an email. She called these four companies, had good conversations with each, and received two assignments on the spot. Lesson learned.

I very much enjoyed the book *Mastering Executive Presence* by Jennifer and John Vautier, which is about career-advancing communication and presentation skills. It is a worthy read.

Good communication takes practice and commitment, and absolutely is a priority. It will greatly help our effectiveness and our relationships.

PRINCIPLES THAT SERVE US WELL AND LEAD TO SUCCESS

- *Lead with humility and empathy.*

- Ask for advice, ideas, honest feedback, and help—this is a sign of strength.

- Humility and excellence go hand-in-hand.

- Be easy to work with, put people at ease.

14

DEVELOP PRODUCTIVE WORKING RELATIONSHIPS

I have done a number of webinars for alumni of Georgetown University. The first was "Earn That Promotion." Following my presentation, I answered questions and then at the end of the hour, I said I hope this discussion was helpful, and that if anyone had additional questions to please email me. Well, I was flooded with questions and every single one of the questions was about their boss: he does not share information with us, he does not give us feedback, he is a micro-manager, he is not helpful, he never shows appreciation, he takes us for granted, and similar issues.

I was taken back by the number of emails received and especially that every single one was about their manager, who they felt was anything but helpful.

Since this webinar and my responses to those emails, I have read numerous surveys by Gallup and others, which validate the magnitude of this problem. About 50 percent of people in the workplace, in industries across the country, feel they do not have a good manager, and about 80 percent do not feel fully engaged in their work, and I could go on. It is clear—and sad—that so often effective leadership is lacking and sorely needed.

It is very important— I would say essential—for us to have good working relationships with our manager and our co-workers. This is in everyone's best interest, and certainly in our company's as well. We will get more done, and done well.

As with just about everything, communication is key. Knowing each other's wants and needs from us is vitally important.

The response I gave to the Georgetown alums following their emails with their concerns, and to hundreds in my leadership and culture coaching and consulting practice since, is as follows; and this goes both ways—to both the manager and her team member, and really to any two colleagues regardless of position and level of authority.

The two should sit down for an individual conversation.

The manager should explain with clarity her team member's specific goals and her expectations, needs, and wants of the team member, that she is here to help her be successful, and to please let her know what she needs to succeed. The two should also discuss and agree upon what good communication between the two of them looks like, such as regular honest and timely feedback, status reports, weekly check-ins, or whatever works for both of them.

If the team member initiates the conversation, she could say that she wants to do her very best work, which is good for the company, the manager, as well as for her, and it is important that she:

- Knows the manager's expectations, needs, and wants from her
- Has clarity of her goals, that they are reasonable, and that she has the resources needed to achieve them

Then she should explain to her manager what she needs from her so that she may do her best work.

Clarity is important. Clearly define expectations, needs, wants, and goals. "Do better" does not work. Be specific.

Stretch goals are fine, just assure that they are reasonable, not close to a miracle to achieve them. Way too often I see top-down goals that are really nearly unobtainable, such as increase revenue by 25% without the resources needed and even, often, with fewer people to help.

I personally prefer a system in which maybe 80% make their goals, versus 10%, which is all too common. After all, making goals is motivating, and an excited, well-motivated team is desirable.

Definitely do not end the working relationship conversation without discussing and agreeing on what good communication looks like between the two of you, such as a weekly individual conversation, or bi-weekly, or whatever will work well and be helpful for each.

This is not too much to ask of a manager. Not at all. After all, conversations are the work of a leader.

I have received appreciative feedback from those who now use this approach. It works if both people are open to developing and maintaining a productive working relationship.

Let's face it,

- It is almost a given that one's manager has to be an advocate for us to advance within our company.
- A leader's priority is to help her people be successful, to help bring out the best in us.

The responsibility to have and maintain productive working relationships goes both ways. The manager has a duty to her people to work well with each of them, and to understand that there is not one way, that each of her team members is unique and may have different needs from her.

Additionally, each team member has a responsibility to work well with her manager, to help her, her team, and her company. Each of us must own our career, and that includes constructive working relationships and communication with our manager and others.

Having positive working relationships applies to everyone. We all want to be easy to work with, to get along, to respect each other, and to help bring out the best in one another.

At a religious retreat recently, the priest spoke about the importance of gratitude—that if we live our life with gratitude for the gifts we are given and the people in our lives, we will be in a positive frame of mind and have a life of contentment and happiness. So true.

I immediately jotted a note, that this also holds very true in business.

The priest also offered that if we are mindful to always say, "Thank you," we are very likely to embody gratitude. Let's commit to that, to say "Thank you" throughout our day.

To reinforce how important this is, just know that more than three out of every four people in business do not feel they are appropriately appreciated for their dedication and work.

Just think how much our sincere thank you's will mean to our colleagues, those of all levels in our company. We could be a beacon of light and warmth. Sure, we all work hard, this is required in the competitive world of business today, and we can still love our work and those with whom we work.

"Feeling gratitude and not expressing it is like wrapping a present and not giving it."

– William Arthur Ward

Live with gratitude and thankfulness without a self-serving purpose, and we can trust that we will be admired and appreciated throughout our company, and we will exemplify good leadership.

Be appreciative and thankful for our colleagues, again of all levels of our company, and likely good things will happen for us all. It is special to work with people we admire, respect, and trust, people we may often consider to be friends.

15

PROMPTLY ADDRESS A PROBLEM OR A DIFFICULT TEAM MEMBER

We cannot correct what we do not confront.

Many of us are conflict-avoidant and would like to duck away from our responsibility to address tough situations involving our colleagues. That said, our addressing problems and having the difficult conversations properly and promptly is our doing the right thing, helping assure our company's positive working environment.

This invariably means stepping up and having a conversation(s) with someone who is a problem.

We owe it to our colleagues and company to have the courage to have the difficult conversation. After all, great teammates and leaders make things better; they do not ignore them.

When we address the problem and the challenges it may involve, we are sending a message to our people that we care about them and our organizational culture.

In general, men are more inclined to try to sweep things under the carpet, hoping they will fade away, while women tend not to tolerate inappropriate and unethical behavior. So, to my fellow guys, let's come out from behind ourselves and sit down with someone who is creating difficulties with team members, and is underperforming, and discuss it. A problem discussed is a problem half-solved—if we approach the situation properly.

Anxiety, angst, and stress do not come from a problem, they come from not addressing the problem and continuing to face it—and the problem will very likely grow worse.

There is an art to having the difficult conversations and we must learn it, as for sure, we'll need it. Problems come with the territory of being in senior positions and having responsibility for and to others.

It helps to write down in advance of our conversation the message we have to deliver, just a few sentences. This is just for ourselves, to prepare for the conversation, what we want and need to say. Make it short and to the point. When we look at it on paper, it is not nearly as difficult to say as it seems when it is living in our head.

Begin the conversation by stating our positive intent and what is at stake.

We need clarity and we must be direct and specific, saying, for example:

- What needs to change.
- By when.
- That we may have contributed to the situation.
- How will successful change be measured.
- That we are there to help.
- The consequence if the person fails to make the necessary change.

Susan Scott's book, *Fierce Conversations: Achieving Success at Work and in Life One Conversation at a Time,* is very helpful in understanding how to initiate and be successful in difficult conversations. This book is a gem.

Think of the conversation as helpful rather than difficult—and it is ultimately helpful to everyone.

A recurring theme in many of my conversations is that their company tends to ignore a problem, incivility, or a difficult team member who is negatively impacting team morale and collaboration. This is frustrating for those who are dedicated and want to do excellent work, individually and as a team. It leads to undue stress, and undue stress at work has become an epidemic.

We will be appreciated and respected by our senior leaders, team members, and other colleagues if we step up promptly to address the difficult issues and/or someone who is toxic to morale.

Leaders make things better!

16

OUR PRESENCE

Are we getting busier—or are we improving?

Our focus is typically on all that we are "doing." We may take pride in all that we are able to accomplish: maintaining long work hours, traveling, being on boards and committees, coaching our kid's athletic teams, volunteering in the community, and the list goes on.

We are constantly "doing." Yet, we are human "beings," not human "doers." It is worth exploring the difference, as this will help us be the best version of ourselves.

At first thought, I viewed our "being" as our fundamental character. Then I realized that we can have a solid character and values and still be caught up in the busyness of the world we live in. Even with the best of intentions, we continue to react to the endless flow of emails, texts, and other demands coming at us.

A leader I greatly admire mentioned that she could spend all day long answering emails, but that she is learning the discipline of making time to stop, sit back, and reflect for even just ten minutes. This allows her to stop reacting and focus on what will truly make a difference in our people's and our company's overall success.

"Being" is elusive. Often there is nothing immediately tangible to show for our time spent simply "being." When we are held accountable for our time, it is hard to justify.

Perhaps the importance of our time spent "being" is better understood in the dynamics that result among our team members, clients, and family. When we spend time just "being" in quiet reflection, the result is nearly always greater intentionality and focus, and more positive and meaningful interactions, conversations, and decisions.

Quiet reflection helps us to be fully present and most effective as leaders. Finding a still place where we will not be interrupted helps us slow down and remember what is so very important: our values and goals as a team member and leader. Sitting quietly and perhaps writing in a journal helps us articulate the values and the qualities we wish to model, the messages we wish to send.

Finding time for quiet reflection and befriending silence can be difficult. One tip is to reflect during times of transition or alone time, for example, when we wake up or retire in the evening or on our daily commute. For President Kennedy, it was time to stand by himself, look out the window of the oval office, and reflect.

Making time for such reflection and self-awareness is vitally important. Without reflection, we charge through our days doing things as they come up. But are they the truly important things, the right things, that we should be doing? Are we having the conversations that really matter?

When we slow down to reflect about who we are as human beings, we can ask ourselves purposeful questions about why we are here, who we are called to be, what our values are, and what will really have mattered when we retire and at the end of our lives.

Some faiths encourage using such times for an honest examination of our self, for example:

- How good a person am I?
- How could I become the best version of myself?
- Am I willing to commit to that?
- Am I making the choices and taking the actions that God would want me to make and do, or I am doing what benefits me?
- What went well today?
- What could I have done better or differently?

While it is most admirable to use these times for reflection about the overall life we are leading, we can also take a little time—even five or ten minutes can be effective—to contemplate our leadership.

During our reflection, we can identify areas that we want to adjust in our leadership, as well as contemplate our relationships and the way we communicate with our team members, and where we truly need to put our focus—on our people.

For example, let's ask ourselves such questions as:

- Am I mentoring and coaching to the best of my ability?
- Am I focused on key priorities, for example, developing trust and constructive relationships, and helping team members learn, grow, and succeed?
- What can I do to connect even more effectively with our people?
- How can I be more encouraging and helpful?
- Am I truly listening and being fully present to others? Or am I often distracted? How can I be more effective with my listening, which is so important?

- As a servant leader, do my satisfaction and success come from the satisfaction and success of my team members?

- How am I striving for my own continuous improvement, as I should be?

- Am I asking for ideas, advice, feedback, and help, realizing that this is a strength?

- What conversations am I avoiding?

- What am I resistant to do? Why?

Genuine inspiration comes from a place of "being," not continuous "doing." This difference is transparent in our work and our leadership.

Reflection also inspires innovative thinking.

We want our actions and conversations to flow directly from our "being."

When we are in a state of "being," we heighten our awareness of those around us, of what is most important. We are cognizant of the dynamics that are going on with team members, clients, and potential clients. We are intuitive and ahead of the curve. In the long run, this saves us time and resources.

When we cultivate a greater ability to be present with others, we are more inclined to truly hear what people are and are not saying. We are more apt to sense verbal and nonverbal expressions of feelings and understand why the person might be feeling as they are. The practice of "being" helps us to quiet our minds and listen without a personal agenda.

Leaders and team members who are present take satisfaction in their team's success, in resolving a challenging situation, or having a difficult conversation. We enjoy when those with whom we work explain how they are striving to be better than before or to share a creative idea that excites them.

Relationships founded on respect and trust for our team members are gifts, as are the genuine conversations that create these relationships. By genuine, I mean when we come out from behind ourselves to be honest, even vulnerable, without putting on airs.

This is important because in business, our very busy schedules can easily dominate our days. Most of us are stretched, and maybe even over-extended and stressed by endless demands on our time and attention and the ever-increasing need to do more and more.

Prioritizing time to "be" is helped when we commit to it by putting it in our schedule and blocking out time each day.

We need to be intentional about reflection. If we don't schedule it, it usually won't happen.

Let's give our work and leadership the attention and time our colleagues deserve. If we don't, we can lose the hearts of our people. They may or may not leave, but they will be less than fully engaged.

No matter what our field, ours is a people business and our relationships are all important. We need to be fully present to develop and maintain these relationships.

Successful leaders are servant leaders. They take the time to be present, to have meaningful, helpful conversations, and to listen without a personal agenda. They understand that relationships with their people are a top priority.

When we take time to simply "be" and reflect on and evaluate our work and leadership and how we are perceived, and then we readjust accordingly, we can be truly influential and meaningful in the lives of the people with whom we work.

PRINCIPLES THAT SERVE US WELL AND LEAD TO SUCCESS

- Aim high, not low, and do not be afraid to take risk.

- Failure is a door we go through to succeed.

- Ask and clarify what success looks like in all our work.

- Respond to people as promptly as possible. This shows our respect.

17

TRY TO ALWAYS BE EARLY

Many years ago, I read a quote "The secret to my success is that I am always 15 minutes early." I typed this on a card that I've carried in my wallet ever since. It has served me well.

I have observed over and over in business just how important timeliness is. It shows our desire and respect. In fact, often when I would arrive early at a business meeting or presentation, I was invariably met with a smile. I firmly believe that being early showed that this really matters to me, that I really care.

The opposite is true. Being late is anything but impressive.

People want to feel respected, as well they should. Being early, or at least punctual, shows our respect for them and for their time.

Of course, there is the very real challenge of the demands on our time and attention. We have to control our schedules so we are able to do the important things, which certainly includes being on time, ideally early, for meetings, other appointments, and delivering our work products.

If we are asked to prepare an analysis, report, proposal, or assignment, we want to deliver it by the due date, if not before. This demonstrates its importance to us.

When I arrive at meetings early, good things usually happen. I have had very helpful conversations. I cannot emphasize this enough. In a number of cases, I really believe that my being early was the difference-maker when things went as I had hoped.

In one case, I had a meeting with a CEO I did not know, who was from out of town. We were to meet in a hotel lobby at 3:30. I arrived at 3:15, as did he. We went into the lounge for coffee and within a few minutes he asked, "How do we do business together?" I was convinced and still am, that my being early really impressed him.

There were times when I would arrive at a client or prospect's office for a meeting early and would be seated outside their office, and a person I was meeting with would appear and we would engage in a social conversation, be it about sports, our background, our family, or where we lived. It helped build rapport. It means a lot when someone wants to do business with us.

This is true for internal meetings, as well. If we are early, which may not be 15 minutes, but even five or ten minutes, we can have good conversations with like-minded colleagues, and the same is true when we do not have to leave immediately when meetings end. This, too, can be an opportunity to connect and build connections.

Trust me, trying to always be 15 minutes early serves us well.

18

MANAGE OUR TIME
AND ATTENTION

Often in these chapters, we mention the hyper-busy world today, certainly in business as well as in our daily lives away from the office. It is easy to be caught up with meetings and calls, and nonstop news when we are at home.

Parents with young children are chauffeurs. The children of so many are barely playing in their neighborhoods; rather they are on travel teams and need to be driven.

In business, it is the endless meetings, which are often too long and ineffective, and the uninterrupted emails and texts coming at us. There is a continuous demand on our time and attention.

These meetings and constant flow of information capture our attention, thereby absorbing us. Many senior executives and their team members and other colleagues tell me that there are conversations and projects they know have very favorable potential and they hope they can get to them sometime soon.

We must not let our schedule manage us; we must manage our schedule so we are doing the right things.

In our church, we pray for the forgiveness of things we have done—and things we have failed to do. Things we have failed to do very definitely include these conversations and initiatives which could make a positive difference for our people—a single person, a team, or everyone in our company, and the potential benefit for our company itself.

We are here on earth to serve others—not to be in conference rooms and in front of our computers and mobile phones for hours on end.

This certainly is not meant to suggest that we work more hours. Not at all. Our personal lives, our family time, time with friends, our faith, and our well-being are truly more important than our work. I believe that—and I also realize being successful in our work is essential, as money does not grow on trees.

It very much helps to be well-organized; the better organized, the better for us. It saves time and helps focus us on priorities.

We must do our part to make meetings more efficient and effective.

There are numerous strategies and resources for managing emails. There is no single solution for everyone, as we all have different circumstances. We each must customize a plan, a strategy, that works for us. We will then be able to have the important conversations and address the priority issues, initiatives, and projects that will help our team members, other colleagues, and our company.

I recommend reading David Allen's book, *Getting Things Done*. I gained a great deal from it.

Success does not simply mean our being busy, it means our doing the right things—that is, helping make things better.

To get ahead, we have to be a hard worker. We have to put in the hours, and we don't count them.

Success in our business means sacrifices, going the extra mile when needed, and pitching in to help others when needed.

These are fundamental principles that serve us well and pay off over the course of our career.

Succeeding in business is not a piece of cake. We must be willing go above and beyond. We need to do what is necessary to help our manager, our teammates, other colleagues, and our company maximize success.

This said, again I believe that our priorities are our faith, family and friends, well-being, and our work, and while we must make sacrifices with hours and travel to serve our clients, meet their needs, help our company's success, we can keep it within reasonable limits.

We should attend our children's birthday parties, ball games, concerts, teachers' nights, graduations, and other school activities, as well as date nights with our spouse or partner—likely not all of them because "business happens," but certainly many of them.

Christine Brown-Quinn wrote a wonderful book, *Step Aside Super Woman: Career and Family for any Woman*. Christine was a managing partner of a financial firm while a wife and a mother of three young children. She states in her book and now in her consulting practice that the key to her success was her laser focus. While at the office, she was all work, giving it 100% attention so she could be home for dinner almost every night. Her firm was competitive so she was focused on getting a great deal done, and done very well, in her eight or nine hours at the office. Others without her focus might take 10 or 12 hours to accomplish what she did daily.

Actually, Christine told me her one regret was that she did not take time to mentor the women coming up behind her. That was her motive to write that book and her next, *Unlock Your Career Success: Knowing the Unwritten Rules Changes Everything*, and she is currently helping a great many younger women with their careers. I highly recommend *Unlock Your Career Success*.

Most companies are family friendly if we are up front about our situation and they see that we are truly "all in" in our effort to help them succeed.

Being well organized is important to our product-fullness. In fact, there is a principle:

For every minute spent organizing, an hour is earned.

A CEO shared how she wished she could do more, that she knows she could make even bigger differences if she had more support. She would like to have more conversations with clients and with her people. Also, she would like to have more time to be out in the community to help raise the presence of the company and the very good things they are doing to serve others.

We discussed options for delegating all except what she has to do personally because of her position.

Actually, she is delegating more and more. However, a problem is her administrative assistant. Simply put, she is not a big help. While a hard worker, she is disorganized, which has been discussed with her, but there has been no real effort to change. Her workspace remains visibly disorganized.

The CEO and other senior leaders seldom ask the administrative assistant for help, as they have little confidence in her delivering what they need.

They like her personally and tolerate it. However, shame on the leaders for permitting this to continue, as it is not fair to the people of the company and their company itself. They need to step up and have the difficult conversation, that change is a must or she will have to find something else to do.

Being organized sets a good impression. Not being organized is anything but impressive.

Whatever our position, we want be orderly and efficient.

Being well-organized should not be that difficult, and there are lots of resources to help. It just requires our commitment to do so.

It is easy to say become well-organized, and it is certainly not easy for a person who has lived her life like this, but if we have ambition to succeed in business, do ourselves and our colleagues a favor and start today to be organized with a dedication to continue to do so.

To advance in our careers, people need to have confidence in us.

19

OUR PRODUCTIVITY IN MEETINGS

No matter what role we play in a meeting, how we show up in that role is critical to the meeting's success.

– Emily M. Axelrod

In a lot of businesses, we spend a great deal of time in meetings. Whether this time is well spent depends.

Here are best practices:

- Are the right people, and only the right people, at the meeting?

- Does the meeting have a defined objective, and do the attendees know it?

- Is there an agenda distributed in advance, ideally three days in advance, so people may come prepared? Yes, three days in advance, as we must realize that introverts are deep thinkers and need time to prepare their ideas…and introverts very often have the best ideas and the most insight. If no advance agenda, they may not contribute, and that is a loss.

- Are meetings scheduled for a proper amount of time? It is common practice to schedule meetings on an hourly basis, such as from nine to ten, simply because that fits a calendar. Maybe the meeting only needs to be 20 minutes, or 40 minutes, not a full hour. A recent article suggests starting a meeting at 9:10 and ending at 9:55, for example, which allows people to get refocused or take a quick break, as it anticipates that some may have another meeting before or after ours.

- Do meetings start on time? End on time?

- Are minutes distributed following the meeting, ideally a day or so after, while everything is fresh in people's minds?

- Does everyone contribute, having been asked for their ideas and opinions? Too often, it is the same people who do nearly all the talking.

- Is respectful disagreement encouraged, even expected? It should be. Respectful debate is healthy.

- Is there an absolute understanding that once the meeting ends, everyone is in accord and supportive of the discussions and decisions made, including those attendees who are not in accord. Unity is essential.

It is so very important that meetings are efficient and effective. They certainly should and can be.

On the other hand, often meetings drone on, are deadly, and are a waste of time. We must respect people's time. A senior and accomplished financial management executive has an axiom, "We can work, or we can meet." He says this kind of tongue-in-cheek, as he does conduct meetings, and his meetings are purposeful, efficient, and do accomplish their desired objective.

If it is our meeting, let's assure we follow best practices as mentioned above. If we are an attendee, but not the chairperson, let's be mindful of these practices and courteously offer our ideas for meeting improvements going forward and do our best to include everyone in the discussions.

We want everyone to contribute their ideas, have robust and respectful discussions, and to leave meetings united.

We must realize that unity is essential.

PRINCIPLES THAT SERVE US WELL AND LEAD TO SUCCESS

- Listening may be our most important skill, especially if we are open-minded, patient, curious, and eager to understand and learn.

- We want the other person to feel heard and understood.

- We want ideas to flow up, and if we want something improved, ask the people who are doing that work.

- Encourage open and honest conversations, and respectful disagreement.

20

INTROVERTS—THEIR INSIGHT IS NEEDED

All too often conversations and meetings end without having everyone's ideas—and maybe the most insightful ideas.

My insightful friend, Andy Funt, gave me the book *Quiet: The Power of Introverts in a World That Can't Stop Talking* by Susan Cain. He said that in my work as a leadership consultant and coach, I should understand how introverts process information, think, and contribute. Susan Cain points out that introverts have so much to contribute as they tend to be deep thinkers. Too often meetings end without their ideas, which could have been especially meaningful.

I was embarrassed that I had never given sufficient thought to introversion. In fact, when Andy told me he is an introvert, I was surprised. However, after reading *Quiet* and being more aware and observant, I believe I keenly understand the need to change modus operandi so introverts are included and able to contribute their insight.

My wife, Kerry, is an introvert and has amazing intuition and astuteness.

Being deep thinkers, it is important that introverts have agendas for meetings in advance, like three days in advance, so they may come to meetings prepared to contribute.

Oh, do I wish I had understood Cain's messages throughout my business career and my personal life.

Shortly after reading *Quiet*, in a discussion with Abby Wilhelm, who at the time was a senior at Hope College in Michigan and is now with a law firm in Washington, D.C., Abby told me how she learned to partner most effectively with someone who is an introvert.

Abby served as an Orientation Director at her college along with another student, Audrey. Among their responsibilities was to meet throughout the summer with campus staff, faculty, and administration to plan for New Student Orientation in August.

Abby knew from earlier conversations that she was an extrovert and Audrey an introvert, but they did not know what that meant in their work together, until they realized that meetings were not running as smoothly as they would have liked. Being an extrovert, Abby was typically the first to fill in pauses, to answer questions, and to direct the conversation. That was how she best processed situations. Being conscious of the fact that she was consuming most of the talking time, she would turn to her co-director during the meetings and ask her if she had anything to add. After a few times of doing this during meetings, Audrey kindly asked Abby to stop. Initially, Abby was confused because she thought she was being considerate by giving Audrey room to speak. What Abby did not realize is that because Audrey was an introvert, she was processing things differently and that it put her in uncomfortable situations when forced to speak on command.

In turn, they restructured their entire approach to meetings so that they could both contribute in their own unique ways. They set aside time before each meeting to discuss their objectives and what topics each felt most comfortable addressing. They also set aside time after each meeting to review how it went. They found this approach gave them boundaries as to when each should speak and it gave Audrey the opportunity to express her insight after she had time to think it over and process it.

Not only did this make the meetings run smoothly, but it also helped them work more effectively as a team in other responsibilities within the student government. They appeared and performed much more unified when they took time to have conversations about their leadership styles.

I was so impressed that these two college seniors figured out on their own how they could be a true team. I am embarrassed to say that until I read *Quiet* I had not thought about or realized how to help an introvert maximize her contributions, and that her contributions may very well be especially important and meaningful.

Understanding introverts (and other personalities) is really important. Nearly half of our population has degrees of introversion.

Once I realized that introverts are deep thinkers and take their time in doing so, I reflected back on meetings. How often it is the same people who speak out, do most of the talking. As Susan Cain points out in her book, all too often meetings end without having everyone's ideas—and maybe the most insightful ideas are missed.

21

THE IMPORTANCE OF NETWORKING

Networking has been cited as the number one unwritten rule of success in business. Who you know really impacts what you know.

– Sallie Krawcheck

It is very helpful to have relationships with people who make things happen and are leaders within our own company, within our industry, and in the business world in general.

I had just completed the manuscript for this book when I read Christine Brown-Quinn's *Unlock Your Career Success: Knowing the Unwritten Rules Changes Everything.* I know Christine, think highly of her and her insight, and was eager to read this.

I am so glad I did, as Christine discusses the importance of networking and the value it brings us.

I had not included networking as an important principle in my first draft of my manuscript. I spoke repeatedly about relationships, that they are critical, but had not addressed the value of networking within and outside our company and in the business world in general. In reflecting back on my own career and those with whom I am close, I realize that there definitely is enormous value in being connected with a wide variety of successful and insightful people.

First, let me be clear that I am not suggesting that we "play up to" important executives in our company. Rather, we should get to know some of them based on our work and their areas of responsibility, where our interests naturally align, and what we know and do may be helpful to them—for example, what we see in our work and/or in the marketplace, client needs and wants, what we see our competitors doing, potential new services, products, and other opportunities.

To advance within our company, we of course need an advocate(s) and we also need visibility within the level of the decision-makers. So, being known as someone who does good work, is a team player, as well as someone who takes initiative, makes things happen, and makes things better is very important.

It may take courage for some of us to network, and let's bear in mind that if we want to advance and be successful in business, we often must be ready to call on our mettle. This is a given.

Having relationships within our industry and the overall business world will only expand our knowledge base, as in having a sense on what our competitors are doing and best practices in general.

Having this knowledge will only make us more valuable within the level of our company that thinks about strategy going forward.

Christine also points out that we well may be able to suggest an ideal candidate to fill an important need of our company, and this will be appreciated.

There is a discussion in *Unlock Your Career Success* about suggested approaches when networking, specifically what we might initially say and how important that is. For example, if when first meeting someone who asks what do I do, I would likely not gain their interest by saying "I am a leadership coach" versus "I founded Common Sense Leadership, as I want to help senior executives improve leadership, their own and their team's."

Christine points out the great value of introducing ourselves with our "Why," not what we do.

I recommend reading *Unlock Your Career Success*. While the book was written to help women in business with their uphill battles in the male-dominated business environment, it is also a worthy read for men, I assure you.

I think women are really good at making friends and not good at networking. Men are good at networking and not necessarily making friends. That's a gross generalization, but I think it holds in many ways.

– Madeleine Albright

22

LET'S MAKE GOOD
THINGS HAPPEN

I wrote this book intending for CEOs, other senior leaders, mid-level managers, up-and-comers, and all those who aspire to be successful in business to reflect on the ideas offered and to help them and their co-workers put into practice the principles that resonate with them.

I also hope to inspire those who may be hesitant to step up and out, to share their ideas, to contribute at meetings, to be visible, and to take risks as appropriate to advance in their careers and reach their potential.

Being successful in business is demanding. There is no easy way. It requires excellence, dedication, hard work, at times sacrifices and long hours, admirable character values, and being a great teammate. This said, we can be successful if we commit to it, and we do not have to do it at the expense of our family and our well-being.

I encourage working with these leadership and team member principles early in our careers as a first impression lasts a lifetime, and these principles take practice to become ingrained in us.

Also, when someone in business is working on changes to improve, even if the person is making good progress, it can take a long time to change the perception of others.

Regardless of our age, it surely is productive and satisfying to always try to be better than before, to be striving to become the best version of ourselves.

Having humility is to know we may be good at what we do, and to know that we can improve. Each of us can.

We need to do excellent work, help others do excellent work, be a great teammate, have constructive working relationships up and down our company and most certainly with our manager, and have a growing network of people we admire. It is very likely that if we are to advance, almost certainly our manager must be an advocate for us.

We must have courage to be comfortable being uncomfortable, initiating the difficult conversation to promptly address a problem and a person who is the cause. We will be respected when we do, and lose respect when we do not.

And we must have the courage to take risks, to speak up, and to ask for the important and challenging assignments. We cannot wait until we feel we are ready. That could well be too late. Trust our ability to learn while we work.

How we show up matters—our composure, our likability, our appearance, our being prepared, being punctual, asking purposeful questions, and listening to learn and understand.

We want to honor others, smile, remember and use their names, treat them with warmth and dignity, and genuinely care about their well-being.

Let us allow ourselves to be vulnerable, to ask for ideas, input, advice, and feedback. Asking for help is a strength.

What can separate some of us from others is our level of inner confidence. If some have a low level of inner confidence, we pray that they will realize they likely have every bit as much potential as those who are confident. We just need to muster the courage to speak up, to do the right things, to make things better, and to help others and our company be better.

We must believe in ourselves.

Having courage is to think of our desired outcome, for a greater good, the higher ground, and step up and respectfully offer our ideas, volunteer, and take action.

Senior leaders are not going to come looking for us. We have to raise our hand, offer our ideas, help improve our company, help our teammates do excellent work themselves, and we have to volunteer for important assignments. As mentioned, having a network of good people will surely be helpful.

Leaders make things better. We all can make things better.

Taking risk is often warranted, again with the greater good in mind, and failing is fine, as we all fail at times and we learn from it. We can learn from our failures and move ahead to success.

Having a mentor and/or a coach is nearly always beneficial in helping us do the right things.

It may also be helpful to have a support group, like-minded colleagues and friends we may want to share with, who will listen, reflect on what they are hearing, and be encouraging.

Yes, success in business can be demanding and will require sacrifice when needed at times, and we can achieve our goals if we are disciplined, speak with honesty about our circumstances, and lead a good, satisfying, all-around life.

The bottom-line message is for us to do excellent work, help others do excellent work, contribute ideas, be helpful, and help others feel good about themselves.

HELP MAKE THINGS BETTER—and very likely we will have a satisfying and rewarding career.

SELECTED BOOKS TO READ

I mentioned that I encourage leaders and those who wish to be, to read perhaps one leadership book a month. I do, and always come away with ideas and inspiration that will help me personally and that I pass along to those with whom I work. Fortunately, many books today are 150 to 200 or so pages and are easy reads.

Here is a list of some of my favorites, which I believe would be helpful to you and your team members. These are in no particular order. I recommend each of them.

Fierce Conversations: Achieving Success at Work and in Life One Conversation at a Time – by Susan Scott. This is one of my "go to" books. It is a very worthy read for everyone!

Three Vital Questions: Transforming Workplace Drama – by David Emerald. As a review stated, this offers how to live in the solution, not in the problem, and our mindset and work environment will change.

The 100/0 Principle: The Secret of Great Relationships – by Al Ritter. Ritter allows himself to be vulnerable by telling his story about being fired, although he had successful results, as his people did not want to work with him. He learned that one-on-one conversations are essential.

Change Your Questions, Change Your Life: 7 Powerful Tools for Life and Work – by Marilee Adams. There is so much insight and so many helpful ideas. Definitely a worthy read.

When Leadership Improves, Everyone Wins: A Discussion of the Principles of Highly Effective Leadership – This is by me, John Keyser, and I have received much appreciative feedback

Culture Infusion: 9 Principles for Creating and Maintaining a Thriving Organizational Culture – by Kerry Alison Wekelo. An astute discussion of the vital importance of our organizational culture, and ideas and principles to achieve a winning culture.

Unlock Your Career Success: Knowing the Unwritten Rules Changes Everything – by Christine Brown-Quinn. Christine wrote this to help women, as that is the mission of her work now. This will be helpful for men as well. Many great ideas that would benefit all of us.

Emotional Intelligence 2.0 by Dr. Travis Bradberry and Dr. Jeanne Greaves.

*Pearls don't lie on the seashore. If you want one,
you must dive for it.*

– Chinese Proverb

Opportunity dances with those on the dance floor.

God gives us the weather, what we do with it is up to us.

*If you are what you should be, then you will
set the world on fire.*

– Saint Catherine of Siena (1347–1380)

*If we want to advance, don't stay on the sidelines,
step onto the playing field.*

ABOUT THE AUTHOR

John has had a long career in leadership roles with Johnson & Higgins, Marsh & McLennan, the Damon Runyan Cancer Research Foundation, and Georgetown University Medical Center. He has been active with and served on numerous charitable boards. A graduate of Georgetown's Institute for Transformational Leadership, John founded his company, Common Sense Leadership, as he wants to help and support senior executives in business, as well as people in the academic and religious worlds, improve leadership, their own and their team's, and develop and maintain an enthusiastic, positive, and collaborative organizational culture. John is a believer in leading with humility and empathy, that every business is a people business, that, as a leader, our success comes from our helping others be great, and that we must encourage ideas to flow up. He and his wife, Kerry, a clinical psychologist, composer of music for reflection and prayer, and a spiritual director, live in Glen Ellyn, Illinois and Charlevoix, Michigan. This is John's third leadership book. He writes a short article or two every month.